# VISUAL MODELING WITH RATIONAL ROSE 2002 AND UML

# The Addison-Wesley Object Technology Series

Grady Booch, Ivar Jacobson, and James Rumbaugh, Series Editors
For more information, check out the series Web site [http://www.awprofessional.com/otseries/].

Ahmed/Umrysh, *Developing Enterprise Java Applications with J2EE™ and UML*

Arlow/Neustadt, *UML and the Unified Process: Practical Object-Oriented Analysis and Design*

Armour/Miller, *Advanced Use Case Modeling: Software Systems*

Bellin/Simone, *The CRC Card Book*

Binder, *Testing Object-Oriented Systems: Models, Patterns, and Tools*

Bittner/Spence, *Use Case Modeling*

Blakley, *CORBA Security: An Introduction to Safe Computing with Objects*

Booch, *Object Solutions: Managing the Object-Oriented Project*

Booch, *Object-Oriented Analysis and Design with Applications, Second Edition*

Booch/Bryan, *Software Engineering with ADA, Third Edition*

Booch/Rumbaugh/Jacobson, *The Unified Modeling Language User Guide*

Box/Brown/Ewald/Sells, *Effective COM: 50 Ways to Improve Your COM and MTS-based Applications*

Carlson, *Modeling XML Applications with UML: Practical e-Business Applications*

Cockburn, *Surviving Object-Oriented Projects: A Manager's Guide*

Collins, *Designing Object-Oriented User Interfaces*

Conallen, *Building Web Applications with UML, Second Edition*

D'Souza/Wills, *Objects, Components, and Frameworks with UML: The Catalysis Approach*

Douglass, *Doing Hard Time: Developing Real-Time Systems with UML, Objects, Frameworks, and Patterns*

Douglass, *Real-Time Design Patterns: Robust Scalable Architecture for Real-Time Systems*

Douglass, *Real-Time UML, Second Edition: Developing Efficient Objects for Embedded Systems*

Eeles/Houston/Kozaczynski, *Building J2EE™ Applications with the Rational Unified Process*

Fontoura/Pree/Rumpe, *The UML Profile for Framework Architectures*

Fowler, *Analysis Patterns: Reusable Object Models*

Fowler/Beck/Brant/Opdyke/Roberts, *Refactoring: Improving the Design of Existing Code*

Fowler/Scott, *UML Distilled, Second Edition: A Brief Guide to the Standard Object Modeling Language*

Gomaa, *Designing Concurrent, Distributed, and Real-Time Applications with UML*

Graham, *Object-Oriented Methods, Third Edition: Principles and Practice*

Heinckiens, *Building Scalable Database Applications: Object-Oriented Design, Architectures, and Implementations*

Hofmeister/Nord/Dilip, *Applied Software Architecture*

Jacobson/Booch/Rumbaugh, *The Unified Software Development Process*

Jordan, *C++ Object Databases: Programming with the ODMG Standard*

Kruchten, *The Rational Unified Process, An Introduction, Second Edition*

Lau, *The Art of Objects: Object-Oriented Design and Architecture*

Leffingwell/Widrig, *Managing Software Requirements: A Unified Approach*

Marshall, *Enterprise Modeling with UML: Designing Successful Software through Business Analysis*

McGregor/Sykes, *A Practical Guide to Testing Object-Oriented Software*

Mellor/Balcer, *Executable UML: A Foundation for Model-Driven Architecture*

Mowbray/Ruh, *Inside CORBA: Distributed Object Standards and Applications*

Naiburg/Maksimchuk, *UML for Database Design*

Oestereich, *Developing Software with UML: Object-Oriented Analysis and Design in Practice, Second Edition*

Page-Jones, *Fundamentals of Object-Oriented Design in UML*

Pohl, *Object-Oriented Programming Using C++, Second Edition*

Quatrani, *Visual Modeling with Rational Rose 2002 and UML*

Rector/Sells, *ATL Internals*

Reed, *Developing Applications with Visual Basic and UML*

Rosenberg/Scott, *Applying Use Case Driven Object Modeling with UML: An Annotated e-Commerce Example*

Rosenberg/Scott, *Use Case Driven Object Modeling with UML: A Practical Approach*

Royce, *Software Project Management: A Unified Framework*

Rumbaugh/Jacobson/Booch, *The Unified Modeling Language Reference Manual*

Schneider/Winters, *Applying Use Cases, Second Edition: A Practical Guide*

Shan/Earle, *Enterprise Computing with Objects: From Client/Server Environments to the Internet*

Smith/Williams, *Performance Solutions: A Practical Guide to Creating Responsive, Scalable Software*

Stevens/Pooley, *Using UML, Updated Edition: Software Engineering with Objects and Components*

Unhelkar, *Process Quality Assurance for UML-Based Projects*

van Harmelen, *Object Modeling and User Interface Design: Designing Interactive Systems*

Warmer/Kleppe, *The Object Constraint Language: Precise Modeling with UML*

White, *Software Configuration Management Strategies and Rational ClearCase®: A Practical Introduction*

# The Component Software Series

Clemens Szyperski, Series Editor
For more information, check out the series Web site [http://www.awprofessional.com/csseries/].

Allen, *Realizing eBusiness with Components*

Atkinson/Bayer/Bunse/Kamsties/Laitenberger/Laqua/Muthig/Paech/Wust/Zettel, *Component-Based Product Line Engineering with UML*

Cheesman/Daniels, *UML Components: A Simple Process for Specifying Component-Based Software*

Szyperski, *Component Software, Second Edition: Beyond Object-Oriented Programming*

Whitehead, *Component-Based Development: Principles and Planning for Business Systems*

# VISUAL MODELING WITH RATIONAL ROSE 2002 AND UML

TERRY QUATRANI

**ADDISON-WESLEY**

Boston • San Francisco • New York
Toronto • Montreal • London • Munich
Paris • Madrid • Capetown • Sydney
Tokyo • Singapore • Mexico City

The publisher offers discounts on this book when ordered in quantity for bulk purchases and special sales. For more information, please contact:

U.S. Corporate and Government Sales
(800) 382-3419
corpsales@pearsontechgroup.com

For sales outside of the U.S., please contact:

International Sales
(317) 581-3793
international@pearsontechgroup.com

Visit Addison-Wesley on the Web: www.awprofessional.com

*Library of Congress Cataloging-in-Publication Data*
Quatrani, Terry.
    Visual modeling with Rational Rose 2002 and UML / Terry Quatrani.
       p. cm.
    ISBN 0-201-72932-6 (pbk. : alk. paper)
    1. Visual programming (Computer science)   2. Object-oriented methods
(Computer science)   3. UML (Computer science)   I. Title.

    QA76.65 .Q39 2003
    006.6'6—dc21                            2002027847

ISBN 0-201-72932-6
Text printed on recycled paper
1 2 3 4 5 6 7 8 9 10—CRS—06 05 04 03 02
First printing, October 2002

# DEDICATION

TO MY HUSBAND, ERNIE,
AND MY SONS, MIKE, MATT, AND STEVE
FOR THEIR LOVE, PATIENCE, AND SUPPORT
AS MOM SPENT YET ANOTHER NIGHT
IN FRONT OF HER COMPUTER.


I WOULD ALSO LIKE TO THANK ALEX BARAN,
WHO MANY YEARS AGO PROMISED ME FAME AND
FORTUNE. I FIGURE THIS BOOK AND ITS TWO PREDECESSORS
TAKE CARE OF THE FAME PART. I AM STILL
WAITING FOR THE FORTUNE PART
TO COME TRUE.

# Contents

# Foreword

Edward Tufte, in his seminal work, *The Visual Display of Quantitative Information,* notes that "graphics reveal data." What he means by this statement is that certain complex sets of data, when visualized graphically, convey far more information to the reader than the raw data itself. So it is with software; as our industry continues to develop systems of greater and greater complexity our ability to manage that complexity follows our ability to visualize our systems above the level of their raw lines of code. Indeed, the market success of languages such as Visual Basic (for which there are more developers than any other programming language, even COBOL) and visual front ends to C++ and Java point out that visualization is essential to the development of complex systems. With the advent of distributed and concurrent systems of all kinds, and especially of web-based systems, the need for visualization of software has never been greater.

As Terry Quatrani writes, her book is "an introduction to the concepts needed to visualize a software system—a process, a notation, and a modeling tool." As I said in the foreword to Terry's first edition, it's clear that these three key components of software development continue to mature and multiply. Today, developers have an even wider range of tools to assist in every aspect of the software development process than they had just two years ago. Furthermore, standards in methods, languages, and tools have begun to emerge and gain widespread adoption, allowing the industry to focus cycle time on actually developing and deploying complex software systems, rather than being distracted by the method wars of the past. Though much debate still continues over languages, I have been privileged to participate in this ongoing process of standardization, not only in the development of the Unified Modeling Language (UML) but recently in the move towards a standard development process initiated, as was UML, within Rational Software. It's been gratifying to see the widespread industry support and acceptance of

the UML and the growing popularity of Rational Rose, the Rational
Suites, and now the Rational Unified Process. As our industry faces
the challenges of building large-scale distributed object applications,
the use of common tools and methods and industry-wide standards
offers the promise of achieving the true interoperability and reuse
of software long sought.

Terry has been working with Rational Rose and the UML
almost from its inception. Her knowledge and experience of methods is extensive, and she has been a driving force in the training
and mentoring of Rational's customers on the use of the UML. This
book is an extension of her everyday work and clearly reflects her
pragmatic knowledge of these subjects and the insights that she has
gained from working on a multitude of complex software systems.
Developers seeking guidance in visualizing a software system will
learn from Terry how to specify, visualize, document, and create a
software solution using the industry's leading tools and methods, all
expressed in standard notation. I've enjoyed the benefits of Terry's
experience and insight for years; I know you will too.

Grady Booch

# Preface

## GOALS

WHEN I SET OUT to write the first version of this book, I thought, "This should be pretty easy... I do this for a living." Boy, was I wrong! Putting into words what I do on a daily basis was one of the hardest things I have ever done (all right, childbirth was more painful, but not by much). But I persevered, spent many, many nights and weekends in front of my computer, and gave birth to *Visual Modeling with Rational Rose and UML.* I must admit that the first time I saw my book on the bookshelf at a local bookstore, I was thrilled. I also found out that you need to have very thick skin to read book reviews. My book is unique since people seem to love it (5 stars) or they are less than impressed with it (1 star). For some reason, I rarely get a rating in between.

I have also figured out that writing a book that is tied to a tool is like rearing a child—it needs constant care. So, once again, I have spent hours in front of my computer updating my book to adhere to the features found in Rational Rose 2002. And no, writing it has not gotten much easier.

As far as the two camps of reviewers, nothing will change there. If you liked the first two versions, you will like this one since the goal of the book has not changed: to be a simple introduction to the world of visual modeling. If you were less than impressed with the first two versions, you will probably not like this version either. It is not a complete guide to the UML (these books have been written by Grady and Jim and I am not even going to attempt to compete with the definitive experts). It is not a complete guide to the Rational Unified Process (these books have been written, quite nicely, by Philippe and Ivar). It is not even a good book on C++ (in fact, I usually tell people that I no longer write code for a living, and there is a very good reason that I don't). As I stated, this book is meant to take a simple, first look at how a process, a language, and a tool may be used to create a blueprint of your system.

## APPROACH

THIS BOOK TAKES a practical approach to teaching visual modeling techniques and the UML. It uses a case study to show the analysis and design of an application. The application is a course registration system for a university. This problem domain was chosen because it is understood easily and is not specific to any field of computer science. You can concentrate on the specifics of modeling the domain rather than investing time in understanding an unfamiliar problem domain.

The problem is treated seriously enough to give you practical exercise with visual modeling techniques and the feeling for solving a real problem, without being so realistic that you are bogged down in details. Thus many interesting and perhaps necessary requirements, considerations, and constraints were put aside to produce a simplified, yet useful case study fitting the scope of this book.

For additional details on visual modeling and the UML or on applying the techniques to your application, you should consider the training and mentoring services offered by Rational Software Corporation. Details may be found at the Rational website: www.rational.com.

## CHAPTER SUMMARIES

THE ORDERING AND number of chapters in this version of the book have not been changed, but the content of the chapters has been updated. The screen shots and Rational Rose instructions have been changed so they reflect what you will see with Rational Rose 2002.

### Chapter 1: Introduction
Introduces the techniques, language, and process that are used throughout the book. This chapter discusses the benefits of visual modeling, the history of the UML, and the software development process used.

## Chapter 2: Beginning a Project
Contains information that is related to the Course Registration
System case study that is used throughout the book.

## Chapter 3: Creating Use Cases
Discusses the techniques used to examine system behavior from
a use-case approach.

## Chapter 4: Finding Classes
Discusses the concepts and notations used for finding objects and
classes. This chapter also discusses the UML concepts of stereotypes
and packages.

## Chapter 5: Discovering Object Interaction
Discusses the addition of scenarios to the system to describe how use
cases are realized as interactions among societies of objects. This
chapter also examines how sequence diagrams and collaboration
diagrams may be used to capture scenarios.

## Chapter 6: Specifying Relationships
Illustrates the definition of relationships between classes in the
system. Specifically, the concepts of association and aggregation
are explored.

## Chapter 7: Adding Behavior and Structure
Shows how the needed structure and behavior of classes are added
to the model under development.

## Chapter 8: Discovering Inheritance
Illustrates the application of generalization and specialization
principles to discover superclass/subclass relationships.

## Chapter 9: Analyzing Object Behavior
Uses Harel state transition diagrams to provide additional analysis
techniques for classes with significant dynamic behavior.

### Chapter 10: Checking the Model

Discusses techniques used to blend and check models for consistency. These techniques are needed when different teams are working on a single project in parallel.

### Chapter 11: Designing the System Architecture

Contains an introduction to the concepts and notation needed to specify and document the system architecture. This chapter is not meant to be a tell-all process guide to the development of the architecture—it is meant to be a guide to the notation and process used to specify, visualize, and document the system architecture. It is placed at this point in the structure of the book since the architectural decisions specified in this chapter must be made prior to the information contained in later chapters.

### Chapter 12: Building the Iterations

Discusses the iteration planning process. It also looks at the UML notation used to specify and document the design decisions that occur during the implementation of an iteration. The chapter does not focus on good (or bad) design decisions—it looks at the process and notations used to capture the design of an iteration.

### Appendix A: Code Generation and Reverse Engineering with C++

Provides step-by-step guides to code generation and reverse engineering using the Rational Rose 2002 and the C++ language.

### Appendix B: Code Generation and Reverse Engineering with Visual C++ and Visual Basic

Provides step-by-step guides to code generation and reverse engineering using Rational Rose 2002 and the Visual C++ and Visual Basic languages.

### Appendix C: A Visual Basic Example

Provides a step-by-step demonstration showing how to create and reuse a Visual Basic DLL.

**Glossary**
Provides definitions of terms used throughout the book.

## ACKNOWLEDGMENTS

I WOULD LIKE to thank a number of individuals for their contributions to the content, style, presentation, and writing of this book.

Special thanks to the following people:

Steve Bailey (Tier Technologies), Naveena Bereny, Kurt Bittner, Grady Booch, Jim Conallen, Ed Delio, Lisa Dornell, Matt Drahzal, Maria Ericsson, Jim Ford, Adam Frankl, Scott Frohman, Jim Gillespie, Dorothy Green, Jon Hopkins, Ivar Jacobson, Jason James, Philippe Kruchten, Eric Lipanovich, Peter Luckey, Greg Meyers, Sue Mickel, Laura Mullins, Larry O'Brien, Sylvia Pacheco, Jim Pietrocarlo, Hugo Sanchez, Charlie Snyder, Lynne Steele, Walker Royce, Jim Rumbaugh, Tom Schultz, John Smith, and Dave Tropeano. I would also like to thank my editor Paul Becker, for without his help this book would never have gone to print.

# Chapter 1

# Introduction

## WHAT IS VISUAL MODELING?

VISUAL MODELING IS a way of thinking about problems using models organized around real-world ideas. Models are useful for understanding problems, communicating with everyone involved with the project (customers, domain experts, analysts, designers, etc.), modeling enterprises, preparing documentation, and designing programs and databases. Modeling promotes better understanding of requirements, cleaner designs, and more maintainable systems.

Models are abstractions that portray the essentials of a complex problem or structure by filtering out nonessential details, thus making the problem easier to understand. Abstraction is a fundamental human capability that permits us to deal with complexity. Engineers, artists, and craftsmen have built models for thousands of years to try out designs before executing them. Development of software systems should be no exception. To build complex systems, the developer must abstract different views of the system, build models using precise notations, verify that the models satisfy the requirements of the system, and gradually add detail to transform the models into an implementation.

We build models of complex systems because we cannot comprehend such systems in their entirety. There are limits to the human capacity to understand complexity. This concept may be seen in the world of architecture. If you want to build a shed in your backyard, you can just start building; if you want to build a new house, you probably need a blueprint; if you are building a skyscraper, you definitely need a blueprint. The same is true in the world of software. Staring at lines of source code or even analyzing forms in Visual Basic does little to provide the programmer with a global view of a development project. Constructing a model allows the designer to focus on the big picture of how a project's components interact, without having to get bogged down in the specific details of each component.

Increasing complexity, resulting from a highly competitive and ever-changing business environment, offers unique challenges to system developers. Models help us organize, visualize, understand,

and create complex things. They are used to help us meet the challenges of developing software today and in the future.

## THE TRIANGLE FOR SUCCESS

I HAVE OFTEN used the triangle for success as shown in Figure 1-1 to explain the components needed for a successful project. You need all three facets—a notation, a process, and a tool. You can learn a notation, but if you don't know how to use it (process), you will probably fail. You may have a great process, but if you can't communicate the process (notation), you will probably fail. And lastly, if you cannot document the artifacts of your work (tool), you will probably fail.

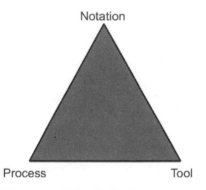

**Figure 1-1    Triangle for Success**

## THE ROLE OF NOTATION

NOTATION PLAYS AN important part in any model—it is the glue that holds the process together. "Notation has three roles:

- ■ It serves as the language for communicating decisions that are not obvious or cannot be inferred from the code itself.

- ■ It provides semantics that are rich enough to capture all important strategic and tactical decisions.

- It offers a form concrete enough for humans to reason and for tools to manipulate."[1]

The Unified Modeling Language (UML) provides a very robust notation, which grows from analysis into design. Certain elements of the notation (for example, classes, associations, aggregations, inheritance) are introduced during analysis. Other elements of the notation (for example, containment implementation indicators and properties) are introduced during design.

## HISTORY OF THE UML

DURING THE 1990s many different methodologies, along with their own set of notations, were introduced to the market. Three of the most popular methods were OMT (Rumbaugh), Booch, and OOSE (Jacobson). Each method had its own value and emphasis. OMT was strong in analysis and weaker in the design area. Booch 1991 was strong in design and weaker in analysis. Jacobson was strong in behavior analysis and weaker in the other areas.

As time moved on, Booch wrote his second book, which adopted a lot of the good analysis techniques advocated by Rumbaugh and Jacobson, among others. Rumbaugh published a series of articles that have become known as OMT-2 that adopted a lot of the good design techniques of Booch. The methods were beginning to converge but they still had their own unique notations. The use of different notations brought confusion to the market since one symbol meant different things to different people. For example, a filled circle was a multiplicity indicator in OMT and an aggregation symbol in Booch. You will hear the term "method wars" being used to describe this period of time—is a class a cloud or a rectangle? Which one is better?

The end of the method wars as far as notation is concerned comes with the adoption of the Unified Modeling Language (UML). "UML is a language used to specify, visualize, and document the artifacts of an object-oriented system under development. It represents the unification of the Booch, OMT, and Objectory notations,

---

[1] Booch, Grady. *Object Solutions.* Redwood City, CA: Addison-Wesley, 1995.

as well as the best ideas from a number of other methodologists as shown in Figure 1-2. By unifying the notations used by these object-oriented methods, the Unified Modeling Language provides the basis for a *de facto* standard in the domain of object-oriented analysis and design founded on a wide base of user experience."[2]

The UML is an attempt to standardize the artifacts of analysis and design: semantic models, syntactic notation, and diagrams. The first public draft (version 0.8) was introduced in October 1995. Feedback from the public and Ivar Jacobson's input were included in the next two versions (0.9 in July 1996 and 0.91 in October 1996). Version 1.0 was presented to the Object Management Group (OMG) for standardization in July 1997. Additional enhancements were incorporated into the 1.1 version of UML, which was presented to the OMG in September 1997. In November 1997, the UML was adopted as the standard modeling language by the OMG. The current version of the UML is UML 1.4 and work is progressing on UML 2.0. You can find more information on the UML by visiting the OMG web site at www.omg.org.

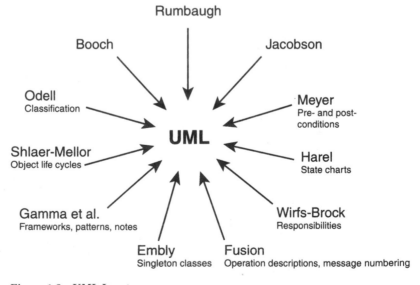

*Figure 1-2    UML Inputs*

[2] *The Unified Method,* Draft Edition (0.8). Rational Software Corporation, October, 1995.

## THE ROLE OF PROCESS

A SUCCESSFUL DEVELOPMENT project satisfies or exceeds the customer's expectations, is developed in a timely and economical fashion, and is resilient to change and adaptation. The development life cycle must promote creativity and innovation. At the same time, the development process must be controlled and measured to ensure that the project is indeed completed. "Creativity is essential to the crafting of all well-structured object-oriented architectures, but developers allowed completely unrestrained creativity tend to never reach closure. Similarly, discipline is required when organizing the efforts of a team of developers, but too much discipline gives birth to an ugly bureaucracy that kills all attempts at innovation."[3] A well-managed iterative and incremental life cycle provides the necessary control without affecting creativity.

## WHAT IS ITERATIVE AND INCREMENTAL DEVELOPMENT?

IN AN ITERATIVE and incremental life cycle (Figure 1-3), development proceeds as a series of iterations that evolve into the final system. Each iteration consists of one or more of the following process components: business modeling, requirements, analysis, design, implementation, test, and deployment. The developers do not assume that all requirements are known at the beginning of the life cycle; indeed change is anticipated throughout all phases.

This type of life cycle is a risk-mitigating process. Technical risks are assessed and prioritized early in the life cycle and are revised during the development of each iteration. Risks are attached to each iteration so that successful completion of the iteration alleviates the risks attached to it. The releases are scheduled to ensure that the highest risks are tackled first. Building the system in this fashion exposes and mitigates the risks of the system early in the

---

[3] Booch, Grady. *Object Solutions.* Redwood City, CA: Addison-Wesley, 1995.

life cycle. The result of this life cycle approach is less risk coupled with minimal investment.[4]

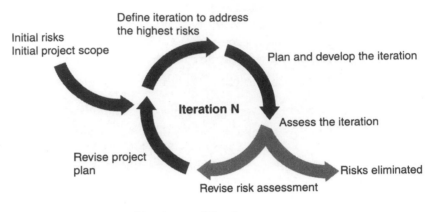

*Figure 1-3   Iterative and Incremental Development*

## THE RATIONAL UNIFIED PROCESS

CONTROL FOR AN iterative and incremental life cycle is supported by employing the Rational Unified Process—an extensive set of guidelines that address the technical and organizational aspects of software development focusing on requirements analysis and design.

The Rational Unified Process is structured along two dimensions:

- Time—division of the life cycle into phases and iterations
- Process components—production of a specific set of artifacts with well-defined activities

Both dimensions must be taken into account for a project to succeed.

---

[4] More information on the application of an iterative and incremental approach to software development may be found in the article "A Rational Development Process" by Philippe Kruchten, *CrossTalk,* 9(7), July 1996, pp. 11–16. This paper is also available on the Rational web site: http://www.rational.com.

Structuring a project along the time dimension involves the adoption of the following time-based phases:

- Inception—specifying the project vision

- Elaboration—planning the necessary activities and required resources; specifying the features and designing the architecture

- Construction—building the product as a series of incremental iterations

- Transition—supplying the product to the user community (manufacturing, delivering, and training)

Structuring the project along the process component dimension includes the following activities:

- Business Modeling—the identification of desired system capabilities and user needs

- Requirements—a narration of the system vision along with a set of functional and nonfunctional requirements

- Analysis and Design—a description of how the system will be realized in the implementation phase

- Implementation—the production of the code that will result in an executable system

- Test—the verification of the entire system

- Deployment—the delivery of the system and user training to the customer

Figure 1-4 shows how the process components are applied to each time-based phase.

Each activity of the process component dimension typically is applied to each phase of the time-based dimension. However, the degree to which a particular process component is applied is dependent upon the phase of development. For example, you may decide to do a proof of concept prototype during the Inception Phase, and thus, you will be doing more than just capturing requirements (you will be doing the analysis, design, implementation, and test needed to complete the prototype). The majority of the analysis process

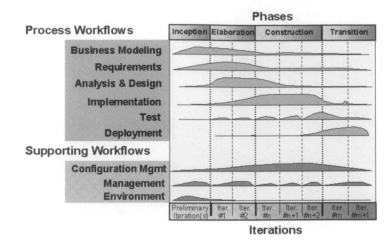

*Figure 1-4    The Development Process*

component occurs during the Elaboration Phase. However, it is also advisable to complete the first few iterations of the system during this phase. These first few iterations typically are used to validate the analysis decisions made for the architecture of the system. Hence, you are doing more than just analyzing the problem. During the Construction Phase of development, the system is completed as a series of iterations. As with any type of development structure, things always crop up as the system is built; thus, you are still doing some analysis.

The diagram is meant to be a guideline for the life cycle of your project. The main point is if you are still trying to figure out what you are supposed to be building as you are writing the code, you are probably in trouble. You should also note that testing is applied throughout the iteration process—you do not wait until all the code is done to see if it all works together!

This book uses a simplified version of the Rational Unified Process, which concentrates on the use of the UML to capture and document the decisions made during the Inception and Elaboration phases of development. The last few chapters lightly cover construction of the system. Although testing is a very integral part of system development, it is beyond the scope of this book.

## THE RATIONAL ROSE TOOL

ANY SOFTWARE DEVELOPMENT method is best supported by a tool. When I first started OO modeling, my tool was paper and a pencil, which left a lot to be desired. There are many tools on the market today—everything from simple drawing tools to sophisticated object modeling tools. This book makes use of the tool Rational Rose. At every step, there is a description of how to use Rational Rose to complete the step.

The Rational Rose product family is designed to provide the software developer with a complete set of visual modeling tools for development of robust, efficient solutions to real business needs in the client/server, distributed enterprise, and real-time systems environments. Rational Rose products share a common universal standard, making modeling accessible to nonprogrammers wanting to model business processes as well as to programmers modeling applications logic. An evaluation version of the Rational Rose tool may be obtained at the Rational Software Corporation website at www.rational.com.

## SUMMARY

VISUAL MODELING IS a way of thinking about problems using models organized around real-world ideas. Models are useful for understanding problems, communication, modeling enterprises, preparing documentation, and designing programs and databases. Modeling promotes better understanding of requirements, cleaner designs, and more maintainable systems. Notation plays an important part in any model—it is the glue that holds the process together. The Unified Modeling Language (UML) provides a very robust notation, which grows from analysis into design.

A successful development project satisfies or exceeds the customer's expectations, is developed in a timely and economical fashion, and is resilient to change and adaptation. The development life cycle must promote creativity and innovation. A well-managed iterative and incremental life cycle provides the necessary control without affecting creativity. In an iterative and incremental development life cycle, development proceeds as a series of iterations that evolve into the final system. Each iteration consists of one or more of the following process components: business modeling, requirements, analysis, design, implementation, test, and deployment.

Control for an iterative and incremental life cycle is provided in the Rational Unified Process—an extensive set of guidelines that address the technical and organizational aspects of software development, focusing on requirements analysis and design. This book uses a simplified version of the Rational Unified Process.

The Rational Rose product family is designed to provide the software developer with a complete set of visual modeling tools for development of robust, efficient solutions to real business needs in the client/server, distributed enterprise, and real-time systems environments.

# Chapter 2

# Beginning a Project

# DEFINING THE RIGHT PROJECT

THE MOST IMPORTANT question to ask when developing a system is not a methodological question. It is not a technical question. It is a seemingly simple, yet remarkably difficult question: "Is this the right system to make?" Unfortunately, this question is often never asked nor answered. Although misguided methodology or technically tough problems can cause projects to fail, sufficient resources and heroic effort by talented people often can save them. But nothing can save a system that is not needed or that automates the wrong thing.

Before starting a project, there must be an idea for it. The process of coming up with an idea for a system along with a general idea of its requirements and form occurs during the Inception Phase. It finishes the statement: "The system we want does . . ." During this phase of development, a vision for the idea is established, and many assumptions are either validated or rejected. Activities that occur involve the solicitation of ideas, the preliminary identification of risks, the identification of external interfaces, the identification of the major functionality that must be provided by the system, and possibly some "proof of concept" prototypes. Ideas come from many sources: customers, domain experts, other developers, industry experts, feasibility studies, and review of existing systems. It is important to note that any prototyping done during this phase should be considered throw-away code since the code generated is merely to support a list of assumptions and has not been fully analyzed or designed.

The process used during this phase of development can be done formally or informally, but it always involves considering the business needs, the available resources, the possible technology, and the user-community desires along with several ideas for new systems. Brainstorming, research, trade studies, cost-benefit analysis, use case analysis, and prototyping can then be performed to produce the target system's concept along with defined purposes, priorities, and context. Usually, a first-pass cut at resource and schedule planning is also done during this phase. For some projects, the product vision can be sketched on the back of a napkin. For others, the product vision may be a formal phase that is iteratively performed until enough level of detail of the target system has been specified.

An adequate Inception Phase establishes the high-level requirements for a desirable and feasible system, both technologically and sociologically. An inadequate Inception Phase leads to systems so unwanted, expensive, impossible, and ill-defined that they are typically never finished or used.

## EASTERN STATE UNIVERSITY (ESU) BACKGROUND

THE ESU COURSE registration problem will be used as an example throughout this book.

The process of assigning professors to courses and the registration of students is a frustrating and time-consuming experience.

After the professors of ESU have decided which courses they are going to teach for the semester, the Registrar's office enters the information into the computer system. A batch report is printed for the professors indicating which courses they will teach. A course catalog is printed and distributed to the students.

The students currently fill out (mulitpart, multicolor) registration forms that indicate their choice in courses, and return the completed forms to the Registrar's office. The typical student load is four courses. The staff of the Registrar's office then enters the students' forms into the mainframe computer system. Once the students' curriculum for the semester has been entered, a batch job is run overnight to assign students to courses. Most of the time the students get their first choice; however, in those cases where there is a conflict, the Registrar's office talks with each student to get additional choices. Once all the students have been successfully assigned to courses, a hard copy of the students' schedule is sent to the students for their verification. Most student registrations are processed within a week, but some exceptional cases take up to two weeks to solve.

Once the initial registration period is completed, professors receive a student roster for each course they are scheduled to teach.

## RISKS FOR THE COURSE REGISTRATION PROBLEM

THE DEVELOPMENT TEAM identified that the major risk to the system involved the ability to store and access the curriculum information efficiently. They developed several prototypes that evaluated data storage and access mechanisms for each database management system under consideration. The results of the prototypes led to the decision that the database risk could be mitigated. Additional prototypes were also developed to study the hardware needs for the university as a result of moving to an online registration system.

## ESU COURSE REGISTRATION PROBLEM STATEMENT

AT THE BEGINNING of each semester, students may request a course catalog containing a list of course offerings for the semester. Information about each course, such as professor, department, and prerequisites will be included to help students make informed decisions.

The new system will allow students to select four course offerings for the coming semester. In addition, each student will indicate two alternative choices in case a course offering becomes filled or canceled. No course offering will have more than ten students or fewer than three students. A course offering with fewer than three students will be canceled. Once the registration process is completed for a student, the registration system sends information to the billing system so the student can be billed for the semester.

Professors must be able to access the online system to indicate which courses they will be teaching, and to see which students signed up for their course offerings.

For each semester, there is a period of time that students can change their schedule. Students must be able to access the system during this time to add or drop courses.

## SUMMARY

THE INCEPTION PHASE is a discovery phase. The problem to be solved is verbalized and discussed among the team and with customers. Assumptions are expressed and may be verified or rejected using proof of concept prototyping techniques. The output of this phase is the identification of the external interfaces, an initial risk assessment, and a set of system requirements. Customers, clients, users, and other interested parties bring various ideas and points of view to this phase and offer the possibility of an early and enthusiastic buy-in.

# Chapter 3

# Creating Use Cases

## SYSTEM BEHAVIOR

THE BEHAVIOR OF the system under development (i.e., what functionality must be provided by the system) is documented in a use case model that illustrates the system's intended functions (use cases), its surroundings (actors), and relationships between the use cases and actors (use case diagrams). The most important role of a use case model is one of communication. It provides a vehicle used by the customers or end users and the developers to discuss the system's functionality and behavior.

The use case model starts in the Inception Phase with the identification of actors and principal use cases for the system. The model is then matured in the Elaboration Phase—more detailed information is added to the identified use cases, and additional use cases are added on an as-needed basis.

## ACTORS

ACTORS ARE NOT part of the system—they represent anyone or anything that must interact with the system. An actor may

- Only input information to the system
- Only receive information from the system
- Input and receive information to and from the system

Typically, these actors arc found in the problem statement and by conversations with customers and domain experts. The following questions may be used to help identify the actors for a system:

- Who is interested in a certain requirement?
- Where in the organization is the system used?
- Who will benefit from the use of the system?
- Who will supply the system with this information, use this information, and remove this information?
- Who will support and maintain the system?

- Does the system use an external resource?

- Does one person play several different roles?

- Do several people play the same role?

- Does the system interact with a legacy system?

In the UML, an actor is represented as a stickman, as shown in Figure 3-1.

*Figure 3-1   UML Notation for an Actor*

### What Constitutes a "Good" Actor?

Care must be taken when identifying the actors for a system. This identification is done in an iterative fashion—the first cut at the list of actors for a system is rarely the final list. For example, is a new student a different actor than a returning student? Suppose you initially say the answer to this question is yes. The next step is to identify how the actor interacts with the system. If the new student uses the system differently than the returning student, they are different actors. If they use the system in the same way, they are the same actor.

Another example is the creation of an actor for every role a person may play. This may also be overkill. A good example is a teaching assistant in the ESU Course Registration System. The teaching assistant takes classes and teaches classes. The capabilities needed to select courses to take and to teach are already captured by the identification of functionality needed by the Student and the Professor actors. Therefore, there is no need for a Teaching Assistant actor.

By looking at the identified actors and documenting how they use the system, you will iteratively arrive at a good set of actors for the system.

## Actors in the ESU Course Registration System

The previous questions were answered as follows:

- Students want to register for courses
- Professors want to select courses to teach
- The Registrar must create the curriculum and generate a catalog for the semester
- The Registrar must maintain all the information about courses, professors, and students
- The Billing System must receive billing information from the system

Based on the answers to the questions posed, the following actors have been identified: Student, Professor, Registrar, and the Billing System.

### CREATING ACTORS IN RATIONAL ROSE

1. Right-click on the Use Case View package in the browser to make the shortcut menu visible.
2. Select the New:Actor menu option. A new actor called New Class is placed in the browser.
3. With the actor called New Class selected, enter the desired name of the actor.

The Browser view of the actors for the ESU Course Registration System is shown in Figure 3-2.

### Actor Documentation

A brief description for each actor should be added to the model. The description should identify the role the actor plays while interacting with the system.

The actor descriptions for the ESU Course Registration System are:

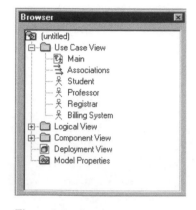

*Figure 3-2   Actors*

- **Student**—a person who is registered to take classes at the University

- **Professor**—a person who is certified to teach classes at the University

- **Registrar**—the person who is responsible for the maintenance of the ESU Course Registration System

- **Billing System**—the external system responsible for student billing

**DOCUMENTING ACTORS IN RATIONAL ROSE**

1. If the documentation window is not visible, open the documentation window by selecting the Documentation menu choice from the View menu.
2. Click to select the actor in the browser.
3. Position the cursor in the documentation window and enter the documentation.

The documentation for the Student actor is shown in Figure 3-3.

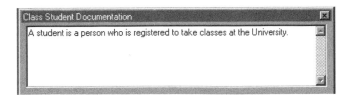

**Figure 3-3  Student Actor Documentation**

## USE CASES

USE CASES MODEL a dialogue between an actor and the system. They represent the functionality provided by the system; that is, what capabilities will be provided to an actor by the system. The collection of use cases for a system constitute all the defined ways the system may be used. The formal definition for a use case is: A use case is a sequence of transactions performed by a system that yields a measurable result of values for a particular actor.

The following questions may be used to help identify the use cases for a system:

- What are the tasks of each actor?
- Will any actor create, store, change, remove, or read information in the system?
- What use case will create, store, change, remove, or read this information?
- Will any actor need to inform the system about sudden, external changes?
- Does any actor need to be informed about certain occurrences in the system?
- What use cases will support and maintain the system?
- Can all functional requirements be performed by the use cases?

In the UML, a use case is represented as an oval, as shown in Figure 3-4.

*Figure 3-4    UML Notation for a Use Case*

### What Constitutes a "Good" Use Case?

Over the years there has been a lot of discussion dealing with the "goodness" of a use case. One problem that I have encountered is the level of detail found in use cases. That is, how big (or how little) should they be? There is no one, right answer. The rule of thumb that I apply is the following:

> A use case typically represents a major piece of
> functionality that is complete from beginning to
> end. A use case must deliver something of value
> to an actor.

For example, in the ESU Course Registration System, the student must select the courses for a semester, the student must be added to the course offerings, and the student must be billed. Is this three use cases, or just one? I would make it one because the functionality represents what happens from beginning to end. What good would the system be if a student was not added to the courses selected (or at least notified if the addition does not occur)? Or if the student was not billed (the University would not stay in business if all courses were free!)?

Another problem is how to bundle functionality that is different but seems to belong together. For example, the Registrar must add courses, delete courses, and modify courses. Three use cases or one use case? Here again, I would make one use case—the maintenance of the curriculum, since the functionality is started by the same actor (the Registrar) and deals with the same entities in the system (the curriculum).

## Use Cases in the ESU Course Registration System

The following needs must be addressed by the system:

- The Student actor needs to use the system to register for courses.
- After the course selection process is completed, the Billing System must be supplied with billing information.
- The Professor actor needs to use the system to select the courses to teach for a semester, and must be able to receive a course roster from the system.
- The Registrar is responsible for the generation of the course catalog for a semester, and for the maintenance of all information about the curriculum, the students, and the professors needed by the system.

Based on these needs, the following use cases have been identified:

- Register for courses
- Select courses to teach
- Request course roster
- Maintain course information
- Maintain professor information
- Maintain student information
- Create course catalog

**CREATING USE CASES IN RATIONAL ROSE**

1. Right-click on the Use Case View in the browser to make the shortcut menu visible.
2. Select the New:Use Case menu option. A new unnamed use case is placed in the browser.
3. With the use case selected, enter the desired name of the use case.

The browser view of the use cases for the ESU Course Registration System is shown in Figure 3-5.

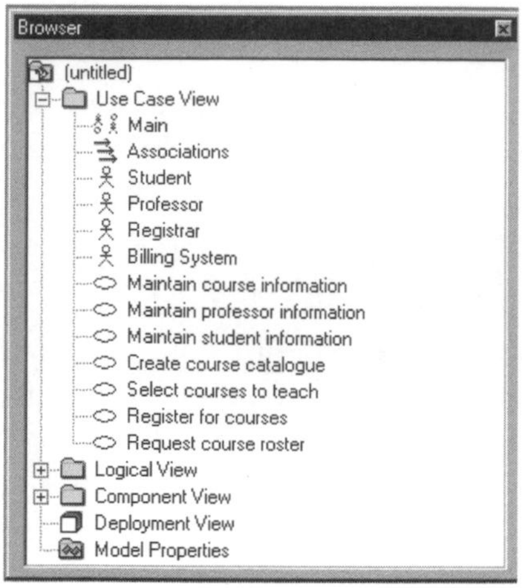

Browser

- [untitled]
  - Use Case View
    - Main
    - Associations
    - Student
    - Professor
    - Registrar
    - Billing System
    - Maintain course information
    - Maintain professor information
    - Maintain student information
    - Create course catalogue
    - Select courses to teach
    - Register for courses
    - Request course roster
  - Logical View
  - Component View
  - Deployment View
  - Model Properties

*Figure 3-5    Use Cases*

## Brief Description of a Use Case

The brief description of a use case states the purpose of the use case in a few sentences, providing a high-level definition of the functionality provided by the use case. This description typically is created during the Inception Phase as the use case is identified.

The brief description of the *Register for Courses* use case is as follows:

> This use case is started by the Student. It provides the capability to create, modify, and/or review a student schedule for a specified semester.

**CREATING A USE CASE BRIEF DESCRIPTION IN RATIONAL ROSE**

1. Click to select the use case in the browser.
2. Position the cursor in the documentation window and enter the brief description for the use case. If the documentation window is not visible, select the View:Documentation menu choice to make the window visible.

The brief description of the *Register for Courses* use case is shown in Figure 3-6.

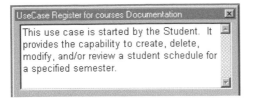

*Figure 3-6   Use Case Brief Description*

### The Flow of Events for a Use Case

Each use case also is documented with a flow of events. The flow of events for a use case is a description of the events needed to accomplish the required behavior of the use case. The flow of events is written in terms of *what* the system should do, not *how* the system does it. That is, it is written in the language of the domain, not in terms of implementation. The flow of events should include:

- When and how the use case starts and ends
- What interaction the use case has with the actors
- What data is needed by the use case
- The normal sequence of events for the use case
- The description of any alternate or exceptional flows

The flow of events documentation typically is created in the Elaboration Phase in an iterative manner. At first, only a brief description of the steps needed to carry out the normal flow of the use case (i.e., what functionality is provided by the use case) is written. As analysis progresses, the steps are fleshed out to add more detail. Finally, the exceptional flows are added to the use case (the what happens if . . . part of the flow of events).

The flow of events for a use case is contained in a document called the Use Case Specification. Each project should use a standard template for the creation of the Use Case Specification. I use the template from the Rational Unified Process.

1.0  Use Case Name

1.1  Brief Description

2.0  Flow of Events

2.1  Basic Flow

2.2  Alternate Flows

2.2.x  < Alternate Flow x >

3.0  Special Requirements

3.x  < Special Requirement x >

4.0  Preconditions

4.x  < Precondition x >

5.0  Post Conditions

5.x  < Postcondition x >

6.0  Extension Points

6.x  < Extension Point x >

A sample completed Use Case Specification document for the *Select Courses to Teach* use case follows.

## Use Case Specification for the Select Courses to Teach Use Case

### 1.0 Use Case Name
*Select* Courses to Teach.

### 1.1 Brief Description
*This use case is started by the Professor. It provides the capability for the Professor to select up to four courses to teach for a selected semester.*

### 2.0 Flow of Events

### 2.1 Basic Flow
*This use case begins when the Professor logs onto the Registration System and enters his/her password. The system verifies that the password is valid (if the password is invalid, Alternate Flow 2.2.1 is executed) and*

*prompts the Professor to select the current semester or a future semester
(if an invalid semester is entered, Alternate Flow 2.2.2 is executed). The
Professor enters the desired semester. The system prompts the Professor
to select the desired activity: ADD, DELETE, REVIEW, PRINT, or
QUIT.*

*If the activity selected is ADD, the system displays the course
screen containing a field for a course name and number. The Professor
enters the name and number of a course (if an invalid name/number
combination is entered, Alternate Flow 2.2.3 is executed). The system
displays the course offerings for the entered course (if the course name
cannot be displayed, Alternate Flow 2.2.4 is executed). The Professor
selects a course offering. The system links the Professor to the selected
course offering (if the link cannot be created, Alternate Flow 2.2.5 is executed). The use case then begins again.*

*If the activity selected is DELETE, the system displays the course
offering screen containing a field for a course offering name and number.
The Professor enters the name and number of a course offering (if an
invalid name/number combination is entered, Alternate Flow 2.2.3 is
executed). The system removes the link to the Professor (if the link cannot be removed, Alternate Flow 2.2.6 is executed). The use case then
begins again.*

*If the activity selected is REVIEW, the system retrieves (if the course
information cannot be retrieved, Alternate Flow 2.2.7 is executed) and
displays the following information for all course offerings for which the
Professor is assigned: course name, course number, course offering number, days of the week, time, and location. When the Professor indicates
that he or she is through reviewing, the use case begins again.*

*If the activity selected is PRINT, the system prints the Professor's
schedule (if the schedule cannot be printed, Alternate Flow 2.2.8 is executed). The use case begins again.*

*If the activity selected is QUIT, the use case ends.*

### 2.2 Alternate Flows

### 2.2.1 Invalid Password
*An invalid password is entered. The user can re-enter a password or ter-
minate the use case.*

*2.2.2 Invalid Semester: The system informs the user that the semester is invalid. The user can re-enter the semester or terminate the use case.*

*2.2.3 Invalid Course Name/Number: The system informs the user that the course name/number is invalid. The user can re-enter a valid name/number combination or terminate the use case.*

*2.2.4 Course Offerings Cannot Be Displayed: The user is informed that this option is not available at the current time. The use case begins again.*

*2.2.5 Cannot Create Link Between Professor and Course Offering: The information is saved and the system will create the link at a later time. The use case begins again.*

*2.2.6 Link Between Professor and Course Offering Cannot Be Removed: The information is saved and the system will remove the link at a later time. The use case begins again.*

*2.2.7 Schedule Information Cannot Be Retrieved: The user is informed that this option is not available at the current time. The use case begins again.*

*2.2.8 Schedule Cannot Be Printed: The user is informed that this option is not available at the current time. The use case begins again.*

### 3.0 Special Requirements
*There are no special requirements for this use case.*

### 4.0 Preconditions
*4.1 The Create Course Offerings subflow of the Maintain Course Information use case must execute before this use case begins.*

### 5.0 Post Conditions
*There are no post conditions.*

### 6.0 Extension Points
*There are no extension points.*

Use Case Specification documents are entered and maintained in documents external to Rational Rose. The documents can be linked to the use case.

**LINKING FLOW OF EVENTS DOCUMENTS**
**TO USE CASES IN RATIONAL ROSE**

1. Right-click on the use case in the browser to make the shortcut menu visible.
2. Select the Open Specification menu option.
3. Select the Files tab.
4. Right-click to make the shortcut menu visible.
5. Select the Insert File menu option.
6. Browse to the appropriate directory and select the desired file.
7. Click the Open button.
8. Click the OK button to close the specification.

Linked documents are also added to the Browser.

A linked use case flow of events document is shown in Figure 3-7.

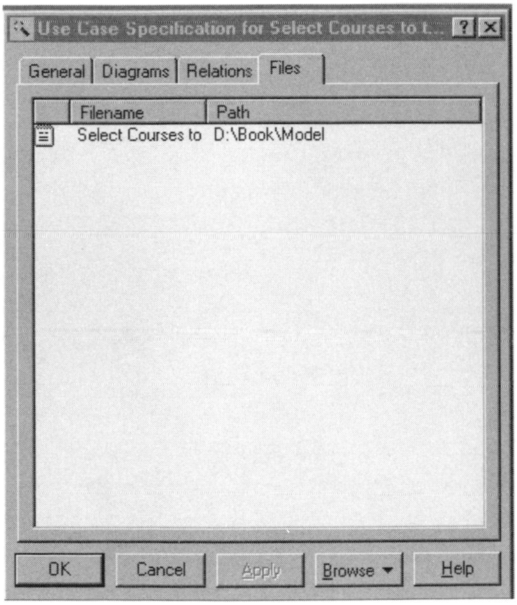

*Figure 3-7   Linked Flow of Events Document*

A Use Case Specification document can also be created in Rational RequisitePro. These documents may also be linked to Rational Rose use cases. To link a RequisitePro document to a use case in Rational Rose you must first associate the Rational Rose model to a RequisitePro project.

**ASSOCIATING A RATIONAL ROSE MODEL WITH A RATIONAL REQUISITEPRO PROJECT**

1. Select the Tools: Rational RequisitePro: Associate Model to Project menu choice.
2. Click the Browse button and navigate to the directory containing the RequisitePro project.
3. Select the project and click the Open button.
4. Click the arrow in the Default Document Type field to make the drop-down menu visible.
5. Select Use Case Specification Document Type.
6. Click the arrow in the Default Requirement Type field to make the drop-down menu visible.
7. Select Use Case Requirement Type.
8. Click the OK button to close the Associate Model to RequisitePro Project window.

The Associate Model to RequisitePro Project window is shown in Figure 3-8.

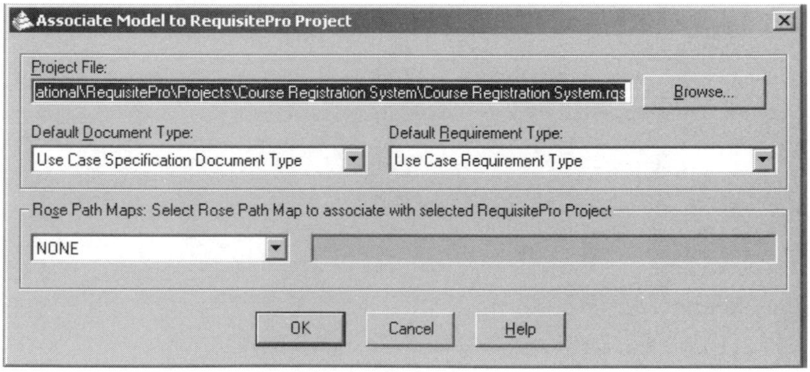

![Associate Model to RequisitePro Project window showing Project File field with "ational\RequisitePro\Projects\Course Registration System\Course Registration System.rqs" and a Browse button, Default Document Type dropdown set to "Use Case Specification Document Type", Default Requirement Type dropdown set to "Use Case Requirement Type", Rose Path Maps dropdown set to "NONE", and OK, Cancel, Help buttons]

*Figure 3-8   Associate Model to RequisitePro Project window*

**LINKING RATIONAL REQUISITEPRO USE CASE SPECIFICATION DOCUMENTS TO USE CASES IN RATIONAL ROSE**

1. Right-click on the use case in the browser to make the shortcut menu visible.
2. Select the Use Case Document: Associate menu choice.
3. Select the Use Case Specification document.
4. Click the OK button to close the Associate Document to Use Case 'Register for Courses' window.

## USE CASE RELATIONSHIPS

AN ASSOCIATION RELATIONSHIP may exist between an actor and a use case. This type of association is often referred to as a *communicate association* since it represents communication between an actor and a use case. An association may be navigable in both directions (actor to use case and use case to actor) or it may be navigable in only one direction (actor to use case or use case to actor). The navigation direction of an association represents who is initiating the communication (i.e., the actor is initiating the communication with the use case, the use case is initiating the communication with the actor). An association is represented as a line connecting the related elements. Navigation in only one direction is depicted by adding an arrowhead to the association line that denotes the direction.

There are two types of relationships that may exist between use cases: *include* and *extend*. Multiple use cases may share pieces of the same functionality. This functionality is placed in a separate use case rather than documenting it in every use case that needs it. *Include* relationships are created between the new use case and any other use case that "uses" its functionality. For example, each use case in the ESU Course Registration System starts with the verification of the user. This functionality can be captured in a User Verification use case, which is then used by other use cases as needed. An *include* relationship is drawn as a dependency relationship that points from the base use case to the used use case.

An *extend* relationship is used to show

- Optional behavior

- Behavior that is run only under certain conditions such as triggering an alarm

- Several different flows that may be run based on actor selection

For example, a use case that monitors the flow of packages on a con-veyer belt can be extended by a Trigger Alarm use case if the pack-ages jam. At this time, no extensions have been identified for the ESU Course Registration System. An *extend* relationship is drawn as a dependency relationship that points from the extension to the base use case.

The UML has a concept called a *stereotype,* which provides the capability of extending the basic modeling elements to create new elements. Thus, the concept of a stereotype allows the UML to have a minimal set of symbols that may be extended where needed to provide the communication artifacts that have meaning for the system under development. Stereotype names are included within guillemets (< <   > >) and placed along the relationship line. Stereo-types are used to create the needed use case relationships. The stereotype < < communicate > > may be added to an association to show that the association is a communicate association. This is optional since an association is the only type of relationship allowed between an actor and a use case. Include and extend relationships must use stereotypes since they are both represented by a depen-dency relationship.

Use case relationships are shown in Figure 3-9.

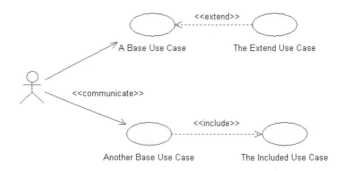

*Figure 3-9   Use Case Relationships*

## USE CASE DIAGRAMS

A USE CASE diagram is a graphical view of some or all of the actors, use cases, and their interactions identified for a system. Each system typically has a Main Use Case diagram, which is a picture of the system boundary (actors) and the major functionality provided by the system (use cases). Other use case diagrams may be created as needed. Some examples follow:

- A diagram showing all the use cases for a selected actor
- A diagram showing all the use cases being implemented in an iteration
- A diagram showing a use case and all its relationships

### CREATING THE MAIN USE CASE DIAGRAM IN RATIONAL ROSE

1. Double-click on the Main diagram in the Use Case View in the browser to open the diagram.
2. Click to select an actor in the browser and drag the actor onto the diagram.
3. Repeat step 2 for each additional actor needed in the diagram.
4. Click to select a use case in the browser and drag the use case onto the diagram.
5. Repeat step 4 for each additional use case needed in the diagram.

Note: Actors and use cases may also be created directly on a use case diagram by using the toolbar.

### CREATING COMMUNICATE ASSOCIATIONS IN RATIONAL ROSE

1. Click to select the Association icon or the Unidirectional Association icon from the diagram toolbar. Note: If the Association icon is not present on the toolbar, it may be added by right-clicking on the toolbar, selecting the Customize menu choice from the shortcut menu, and adding the icon to the toolbar.
2. Click on an actor initiating a communication and drag the association line to the desired use case.

To add the communicate stereotype (optional):

1.  Double-click on the association line to make the Specification visible.
2.  Click the arrow in the Stereotype field to make the drop-down menu visible, and select communicate.
3.  Click the OK button to close the Specification.
4.  Repeat the preceding steps for each additional communicate relationship.

**CREATING INCLUDE RELATIONSHIPS IN RATIONAL ROSE**

1.  Click to select the Dependency icon from the toolbar.
2.  Click on the base use case and drag the Dependency icon to the used use case.
3.  Double-click on the dependency arrow to make the Specification visible.
4.  Click the arrow in the Stereotype field to make the drop-down menu visible, and select include.
5.  Click the OK button to close the Specification.

**CREATING EXTEND RELATIONSHIPS IN RATIONAL ROSE**

1.  Click to select the Dependency icon from the toolbar.
2.  Click on the use case containing the extended functionality and drag the Dependency icon to the base use case.
3.  Double-click on the dependency arrow to make the Specification visible.
4.  Click the arrow in the Stereotype field to make the drop-down menu visible and select extend.
5.  Click the OK button to close the Specification.

The Main use case diagram for the ESU Course Registration System is shown in Figure 3-10.

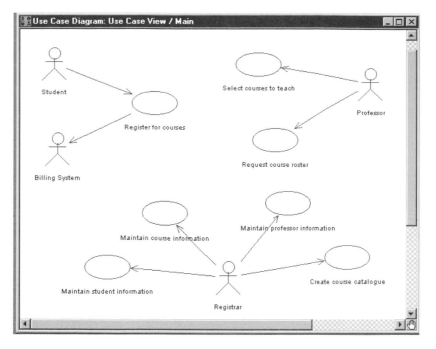

*Figure 3-10   Main Use Case Diagram*

**CREATING ADDITIONAL USE CASE DIAGRAMS IN RATIONAL ROSE**

1. Right-click on the Use Case View in the browser to make the shortcut menu visible.
2. Select the New:Use Case Diagram menu option.
3. While the use case diagram is selected, enter the name of the actor.
4. Open the diagram and add actors, use cases, and interactions to the diagram as needed.

An additional use case diagram is shown in Figure 3-11.

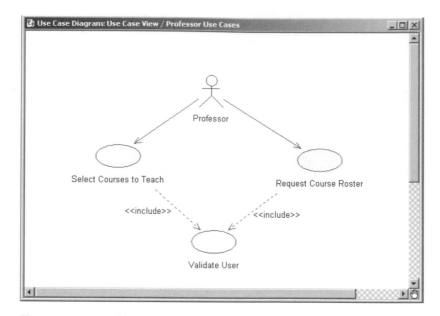

*Figure 3-11   An Additional Use Case Diagram*

## ACTIVITY DIAGRAMS

ACTIVITY DIAGRAMS also may be created at this stage in the life cycle. These diagrams represent the dynamics of the system. They are flow charts that are used to show the workflow of a system; that is, they show the flow of control from activity to activity in the system, what activities can be done in parallel, and any alternate paths through the flow. At this point in the life cycle, activity diagrams may be created to represent the flow across use cases or they may be created to represent the flow within a particular use case. Later in the life cycle, activity diagrams may be created to show the workflow for an operation.

Activity diagrams contain activities, transitions between the activities, decision points, and synchronization bars. In the UML, activities are represented as rectangles with rounded edges, transitions are drawn as directed arrows, decision points are shown as diamonds, and synchronization bars are drawn as thick horizontal or vertical bars as shown in Figure 3-12.

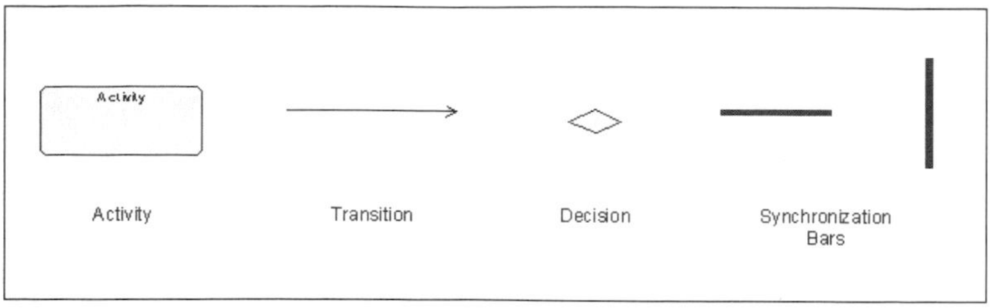

| Activity | Transition | Decision | Synchronization Bars | |
|----------|------------|----------|----------------------|---|

*Figure 3-12    UML Notation for Activity Diagram Elements*

**CREATING ACTIVITY DIAGRAMS IN RATIONAL ROSE**

1. Right-click on the Use Case View in the browser to make the shortcut menu visible.
2. Select the New:Activity Diagram menu choice. This will add an activity diagram called NewDiagram to the browser.
3. While the new diagram is still selected, enter the name of the diagram.
4. Double-click on the activity diagram in the browser to open the diagram.

A browser view of an activity diagram is shown in Figure 3-13.

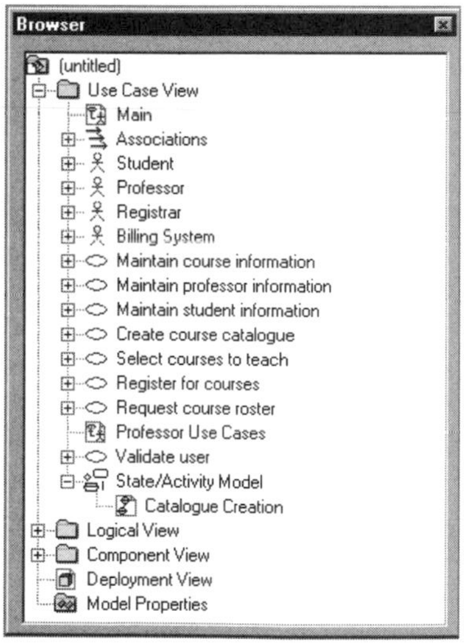

*Figure 3-13    Activity Diagram in the Browser*

## Activities

An activity represents the performance of some behavior in the workflow.

**CREATING ACTIVITIES IN RATIONAL ROSE**

1.  Click to select the Activity icon from the toolbar.
2.  Click on the activity diagram window to place the activity.
3.  While the activity is still selected, enter the name of the activity.

Activities are shown in Figure 3-14.

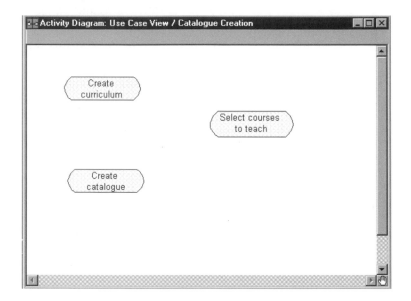

*Figure 3-14 Activities*

## Transitions

Transitions are used to show the passing of the flow of control from activity to activity. They are typically triggered by the completion of the behavior in the originating activity.

**CREATING TRANSITIONS IN RATIONAL ROSE**

1. Click to select the state transition icon from the toolbar.
2. Click on the originating activity and drag the transition arrow to the successor activity.

Transitions are shown in Figure 3-15.

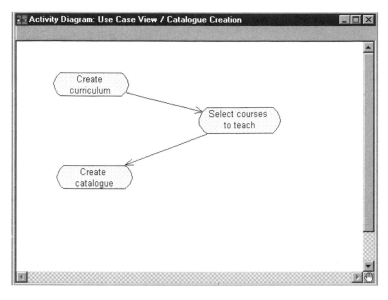

*Figure 3-15   Transitions*

## Decision Points

When modeling the workflow of a system it is often necessary to show where the flow of control branches based on a decision point. The transitions from a decision point contain a guard condition, which is used to determine which path from the decision point is taken. Decisions along with their guard conditions allow you to show alternate paths through a work flow.

**CREATING DECISION POINTS IN RATIONAL ROSE**

1. Click to select the Decision icon from the toolbar.
2. Click on the activity diagram window to place the decision.

3. While the decision is still selected, enter the name of the decision.
4. Click to select the Transition icon on the toolbar.
5. Click on the originating activity and drag the transition to the decision icon.

A decision point is shown in Figure 3-16.

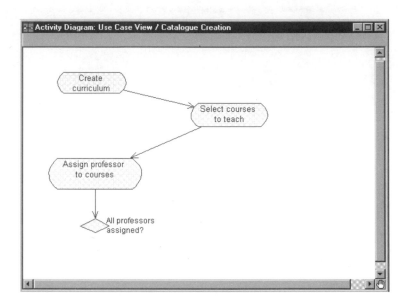

*Figure 3-16   Decision in an Activity Diagram*

 **CREATING GUARDED TRANSITIONS IN RATIONAL ROSE**

1. Click to select the State Transition icon from the toolbar.
2. Click on the decision and drag the transition to the successor activity. (Note: Rational Rose may place the transition on top of an existing transition. To separate the transition, select the transition and drag it onto the activity diagram window.)
3. Double-click on the transition arrow to make the Specification visible.

4. Select the Detail tab.
5. Enter the guard condition in the Guard Condition field.
6. Click the OK button to close the Specification.

A transition with a guard is shown in Figure 3-17.

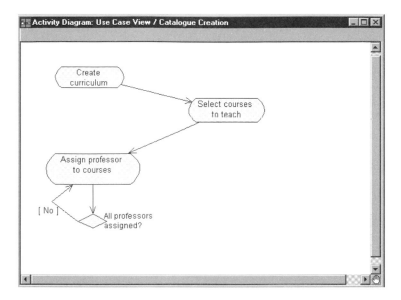

*Figure 3-17 Guarded Transition*

**CREATING RECTILINEAR LINES IN RATIONAL ROSE**

1. Click to select the line that should be rectilinear (multi-select may be accomplished by first selecting the Shift button).
2. Select the Format: Line Style: Rectilinear menu choice.
3. Relocate the lines as needed by selecting the line and dragging it to the desired location on the activity diagram window.

Rectilinear lines are shown in Figure 3-18.

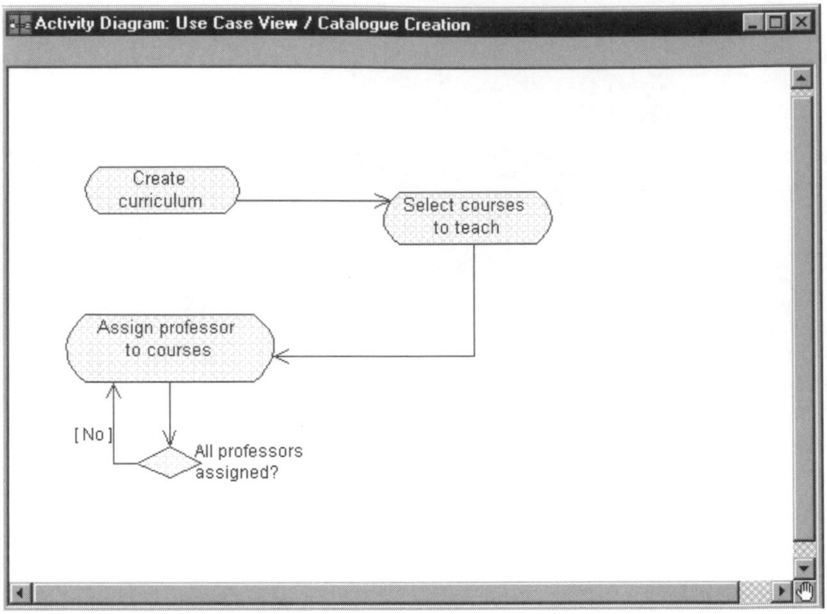

**Activity Diagram: Use Case View / Catalogue Creation**

Create curriculum

Select courses to teach

Assign professor to courses

[ No ]

All professors assigned?

*Figure 3-18   Rectilinear Lines*

### Synchronization Bars

In a workflow there are typically some activities that may be done in parallel. A synchronization bar allows you to specify what activities may be done concurrently. Synchronization bars are also used to show joins in the workflow; that is, what activities must complete before processing may continue. That said, a synchronization bar may have many incoming transitions and one outgoing transition, or one incoming transition and many outgoing transitions.

**CREATING SYNCHRONIZATION BARS IN RATIONAL ROSE**

1.  Click to select the Horizontal Synchronization or the Vertical Synchronization icon from the toolbar.
2.  Click on the activity diagram window to place the synchronization bar.
3.  Click to select the State Transition icon on the toolbar and add any needed incoming and outgoing transitions to the synchronization bar.

Synchronization bars are shown in Figure 3-19.

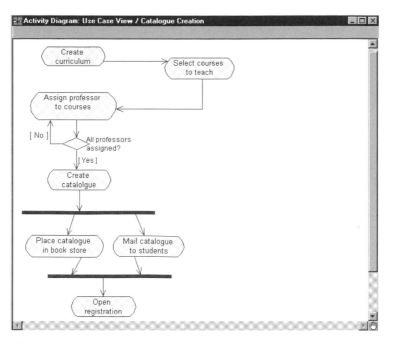

*Figure 3-19   Synchronization Bars*

## Swimlanes

Swimlanes may be used to partition an activity diagram. This typically is done to show what person or organization is responsible for the activities contained in the swimlane.

**CREATING SWIMLANES IN RATIONAL ROSE**

1. Click to select the Swimlane icon from the toolbar.
2. Click on the activity diagram window to place the swimlane. This will add a swimlane called NewSwimlane to the diagram.
3. Double-click on the NewSwimlane (the words) to open the Specification.
4. Enter the name of the swimlane in the Name field.
5. Click the OK button to close the Specification.

6.  To resize the swimlane, click on the swimlane border and drag the swimlane to the desired location.
7.  Drag all needed activities and transitions into the swimlane. (Note: You may also create new activities and transitions in the swimlane.)

An activity diagram with swimlanes is shown in Figure 3-20.

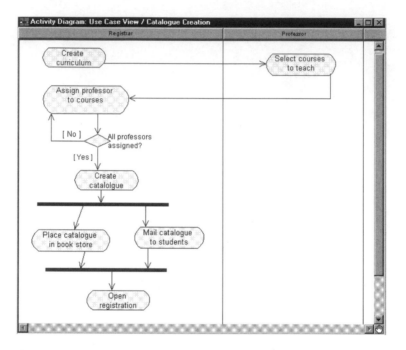

*Figure 3-20  Swimlanes*

## Initial and Final Activities

There are special symbols that are used to show the starting and final activities in a workflow. The starting activity is shown using a solid filled circle and the final activities are shown using a bull's eye. Typically, there is one starting activity for the workflow and there may be more than one ending activity (one for each alternate flow in the workflow).

**CREATING STARTING AND ENDING ACTIVITIES IN RATIONAL ROSE**

1.  Click to select the Start State or the End State icon from the toolbar.
2.  Click on the activity diagram window to place the start or end state.
3.  If you added a start state, click on the State Transition icon, click on the start state, and drag the transition to the first activity in the workflow.
4.  If you added an end state, click on the State Transition icon, click on the successor activity, and drag the transition to the end state.

An activity diagram with start and end states is shown in Figure 3-21.

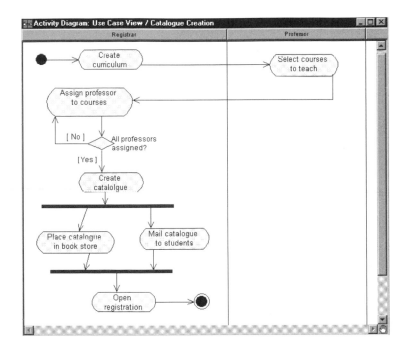

*Figure 3-21  Start and End States*

## SUMMARY

SYSTEM BEHAVIOR IS documented in a use case model that illustrates the system's intended functions (use cases), its surroundings (actors), and the relationships between the use cases and actors (use case diagrams). The most important role of a use case model is to communicate the system's functionality and behavior to the customer or end user.

The use case model starts in the Inception Phase with the identification of the actors and the principal use cases for the system. The model is then matured in the Elaboration Phase.

Actors are not part of the system—they represent anyone or anything that must interact with the system under development. Use cases represent the functionality provided by the system. They model a dialogue between an actor and the system.

Each use case contains a flow of events, which is a description of the events needed to accomplish the use case functionality. The flow of events is written in terms of *what* the system should do, not *how* the system does it. A use case diagram is a graphical representation of some or all of the actors, use cases, and their interactions for a system.

Two popular types of use case relationships are include and extend. An include relationship is drawn to show functionality that is shared by several use cases; an extend relationship depicts optional behavior of a use case.

Activity diagrams represent the dynamics of the system. They are flow charts that are used to show the workflow of a system. At this point in the life cycle, activity diagrams may be created to represent the flow across use cases or they may be created to represent the flow within a particular use case. Later in the life cycle, activity diagrams may be created to show the workflow for an operation.

## Chapter 4

# Finding Classes

## WHAT IS AN OBJECT?

AN OBJECT IS a representation of an entity, either real-world or conceptual. An object can represent something concrete, such as Joe's truck or my computer, or a concept such as a chemical process, a bank transaction, a purchase order, Mary's credit history, or an interest rate.

An object is a concept, abstraction, or thing with well-defined boundaries and meaning for an application. Each object in a system has three characteristics: state, behavior, and identity.

## STATE, BEHAVIOR, AND IDENTITY

THE STATE OF an object is one of the possible conditions in which it may exist. The state of an object typically changes over time, and is defined by a set of properties (called attributes), with the values of the properties, plus the relationships the object may have with other objects. For example, a course offering object in the registration system may be in one of two states: *open* and *closed*. If the number of students registered for a course offering is less than 10, the state of the course offering is open. When the tenth student registers for the course offering, the state becomes closed.

Behavior determines how an object responds to requests from other objects and typifies everything the object can do. Behavior is implemented by the set of operations for the object. In the registration system, a course offering could have the behaviors *add a student* and *delete a student*.

Identity means that each object is unique—even if its state is identical to that of another object. For example, Algebra 101, Section 1, and Algebra 101, Section 2 are two objects in the Course Registration System. Although they are both course offerings, they each have a unique identity.

In the UML, objects are represented as rectangles and the name of the object is underlined as shown in Figure 4-1.

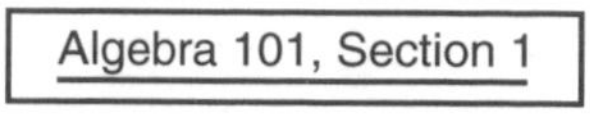

| Algebra 101, Section 1 |
| --- |

*Figure 4-1    UML Notation for an Object*

## WHAT IS A CLASS?

A CLASS IS a description of a group of objects with common properties (attributes), common behavior (operations), common relationships to other objects, and common semantics. Thus, a class
is a template to create objects. Each object is an instance of some
class and objects cannot be instances of more than one class. For
example, the CourseOffering class may be defined with the following characteristics:

- Attributes—location, time offered
- Operations—retrieve location, retrieve time of day, add
  a student to the offering

Algebra 101, Section 1, and Algebra 101, Section 2 are objects
belonging to the CourseOffering class. Each object would have a
value for the attributes and access to the operations specified by
the CourseOffering class.

A good class captures one and only one abstraction—it should
have one major theme. For example, a class that has the capability
of maintaining information about a student and the information
about all the course offerings that the student has taken over
the years is not a good class since it does not have one major
theme. This class should be split into two related classes:
Student and StudentHistory.

Classes should be named using the vocabulary of the domain.
The name should be a singular noun that best characterizes the
abstraction. Acronyms may be used if the acronym has the same
meaning for all involved, but if an acronym has different meanings
for different people then the full name should always be used. If
a class is named with an acronym, the full name should also be
contained in the class documentation.

It is often hard to distinguish between an object and a class. Why is Algebra 101, Section 1 an object and not a class? What makes it different from Algebra 101, Section 2? The answers to these questions are very subjective. By looking at their structure and behavior, it can be seen that both have the same structure and behavior. They are only different course offerings for a semester. In addition, it may be noted that there are many other "things" in the Course Registration System that have the same structure and behavior (e.g., Music 101, Section 1; History 101, Section 1; and History 101, Section 2). This leads to the decision to create a CourseOffering class.

In the UML, classes are represented as compartmentalized rectangles. The top compartment contains the name of the class, the middle compartment contains the structure of the class (attributes), and the bottom compartment contains the behavior of the class (operations). A class is shown in Figure 4-2.

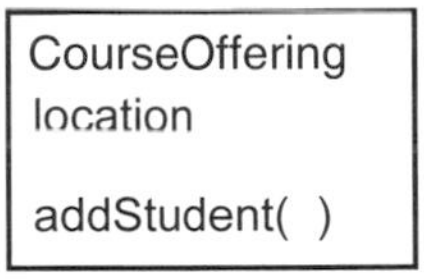

*Figure 4-2    UML Notation for a Class*

**CREATING CLASSES IN THE ROSE BROWSER**

1.  Right-click to select the Logical View in the browser.
2.  Select the New:Class menu choice. A class called New Class is placed in the browser.
3.  While the new class is still selected, enter the name of the class.

The browser view of a class is shown in Figure 4-3.

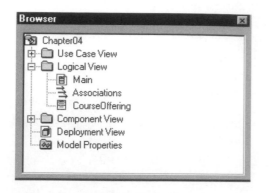

*Figure 4-3   Class Created in the Browser*

## STEREOTYPES AND CLASSES

WE PREVIOUSLY TALKED about stereotypes for relationships in use case diagrams. Classes can also have stereotypes. As before, a stereotype provides the capability to create a new kind of modeling element. Here, we can create new kinds of classes. Some common stereotypes for a class are entity, boundary, control, utility, and exception.

The stereotype for a class is shown below the class name enclosed in guillemets (< <   > >). If desired, a graphic icon or a specific color may be associated with a stereotype. In Rational Rose, icons for the Rational Unified Process stereotypes of control, entity, and boundary are supplied.  These stereotypes are shown in Figure 4-4 along with an example of a class with a stereotype of exception.

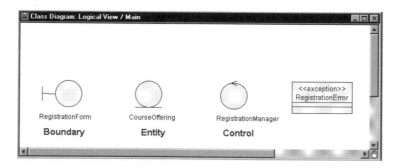

*Figure 4-4   Classes with Stereotypes*

# DISCOVERING CLASSES

A COOKBOOK FOR finding classes does not exist. As Grady Booch has been known to say, "This is hard!" The Rational Unified Process advocates finding the classes for a system under development by looking for boundary, control, and entity classes. These three stereotypes conform to a "model-view-controller" point of view and allow the analyst to partition the system by separating the view from the domain from the control needed by the system.

Since the analysis and design process is iterative, the list of classes will change as time moves on. The initial set of classes probably will not be the set of classes that eventually gets implemented. Thus, the term candidate class is often used to describe the first set of classes found for a system.

## Entity Classes

An entity class models information and associated behavior that is generally long lived. This type of class may reflect a real-world entity or it may be needed to perform tasks internal to the system. They are typically independent of their surroundings; that is, they are not sensitive to how the surroundings communicate with the system. Many times, they are application independent, meaning that they may be used in more than one application.

The first step is to examine the responsibilities documented in the flow of events for the identified use cases (i.e., what the system must do). Entity classes typically are classes that are needed by the system to accomplish some responsibility. The nouns and noun phrases used to describe the responsibility may be a good starting point. The initial list of nouns must be filtered because it could contain nouns that are outside the problem domain, nouns that are just language expressions, nouns that are redundant, and nouns that are descriptions of class structures.

Entity classes typically are found early in the Elaboration Phase. They are often called "domain" classes since they usually deal with abstractions of real-world entities.

## Boundary Classes

Boundary classes handle the communication between the system surroundings and the inside of the system. They can provide the interface to a user or another system (i.e., the interface to an actor). They constitute the surroundings-dependent part of the system. Boundary classes are used to model the system interfaces.

Each physical actor/scenario pair is examined to discover boundary classes. The boundary classes chosen in the Elaboration Phase of development are typically at a high level. For example, you may model a window but not model each of its dialogue boxes and buttons. At this point, you are documenting the user interface requirements, not implementing the interface.

User interface requirements tend to be very vague—the terms user-friendly and flexible seem to be used a lot. But user-friendly means different things to different people. This is where prototyping and storyboarding techniques can be very useful. The customer can get the "look and feel" of the system and truly capture *what* user-friendly means. The *what* is then captured as the structure and behavior of the boundary class. During design these classes are refined to take into consideration the chosen user interface mechanisms—how they are to be implemented.

Boundary classes are also added to facilitate communication with other systems. During design, these classes are refined to take into consideration the chosen communication protocols.

## Control Classes

Control classes model sequencing behavior specific to one or more use cases. Control classes coordinate the events needed to realize the behavior specified in the use case. You can think of a control class as "running" or "executing" the use case—they represent the dynamics of the use case. Control classes typically are application-dependent classes.

In the early stages of the Elaboration Phase, a control class is added for each actor/use case pair. The control class is responsible for the flow of events in the use case.

The use of control classes is very subjective. Many authors feel that the use of control classes results in behavior being separated from data. This can happen if your control classes are not chosen wisely. If a control class is doing more than sequencing, then it is doing too much! For example, in the Course Registration System, a student selects course offerings and if the course offering is available, the student is added to it. Who knows how to add the student—the control class or the course offering? The right answer is the course offering. The control class knows when the student should be added; the course offering knows how to add the student. A bad control class would not only know when to add the student but how to add the student.

The addition of a control class per actor/use case pair is only an initial cut—as analysis and design continues, control classes may be eliminated, split up, or combined.

**CREATING STEREOTYPES FOR CLASSES IN RATIONAL ROSE**

1. Right-click to select the class in the browser and make the shortcut menu visible.
2. Select the Open Specification menu choice.
3. Select the General tab.
4. Click the arrow in the Stereotype field to make the drop-down menu visible and select the desired stereotype or, to create a new stereotype, enter the name of the stereotype in the Stereotype field.
5. Click the OK button to close the Specification.

The Specification for the Student class is shown in Figure 4-5. If the default language for a model is set to a language other than analysis (Tools: Options menu choice, Notation tab), then a tab for that language will be added to the class specification.

## DOCUMENTING CLASSES

AS CLASSES ARE created, they should also be documented. The documentation should state the purpose of the class and not the structure of the class. For example, a Student class could be documented as follows:

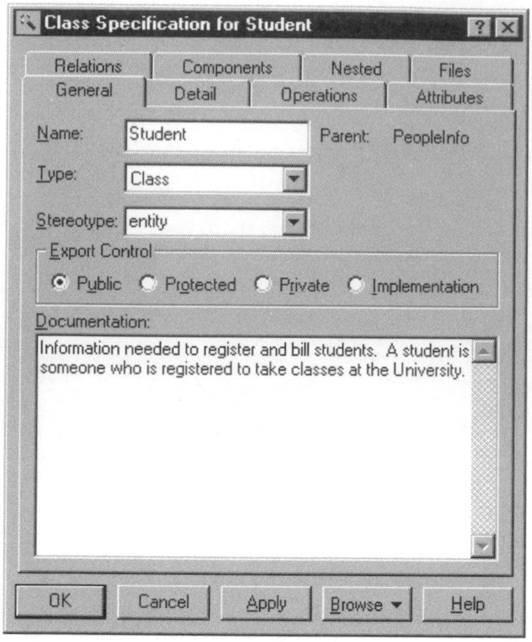

*Figure 4-5   Setting a Class Stereotype*

> *Information needed to register and bill students. A student is someone currently registered to take classes at the University.*

A bad definition would be the following:

> *The name, address, and phone number of a student.*

This definition only tells me the structure of the class, which can be determined by looking at its attributes. It does not tell me why I need the class.

Difficulty in naming or documenting a class may be an indication that it is not a good abstraction. The following list typifies things that can happen as classes are named and documented:

- Can identify a name and a clear concise definition—good candidate class

- Can identify a name, but the definition is the same as another class—combine the classes

- Can identify a name, but need a book to document the purpose—break up the class

- Cannot identify a name or a definition—more analysis is needed to determine the correct abstractions

**DOCUMENTING CLASSES IN RATIONAL ROSE**

1. Click to select the class in the browser.
2. Position the cursor in the documentation window and enter the documentation for the class.

The description of the Student class is shown in Figure 4-6.

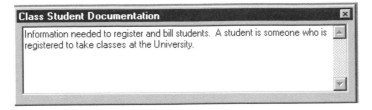

*Figure 4-6   Class Documentation*

## PACKAGES

IF A SYSTEM contained only a few classes, you could manage them easily. Most systems are composed of many classes, and thus you need a mechanism to group them together for ease of use, maintainability, and reusability. This is where the concept of a package is useful. A package in the logical view of the model is a collection of related packages and/or classes. By grouping classes into packages, we can look at the "higher" level view of the model (i.e., the packages) or we can dig deeper into the model by looking at what is contained by the package.

Each package contains an interface that is realized by its set of public classes—those classes to which classes in other packages talk. The rest of the classes in a package are implementation classes—classes do not communicate with classes in other packages.

If the system is complex, packages may be created early in the Elaboration Phase to facilitate communication. For simpler systems, the classes found early in analysis may be grouped into one package—the system itself. As analysis and design progress, the concept of a package will be used to group the classes that are needed to carry out the architectural decisions made for the system.

In the UML, packages are represented as folders. A package is shown in Figure 4-7.

*Figure 4-7   UML Notation for a Package*

**CREATING PACKAGES IN THE ROSE BROWSER**

1. Right-click to select the Logical View in the browser.
2. Select the New:Package menu choice.
3. While the package is still selected, enter the name of the package.

A package created via the browser is shown in Figure 4-8. As packages are created, classes in the model are relocated.

**RELOCATING CLASSES IN THE ROSE BROWSER**

1. Click to select the class in the browser.
2. Drag the class to the desired package.
3. Repeat the steps for each class that is to be relocated.

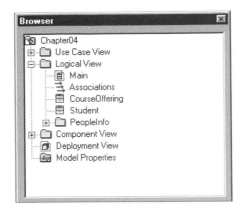

*Figure 4-8   Package Created in the Browser*

Relocated classes are shown in Figure 4-9.

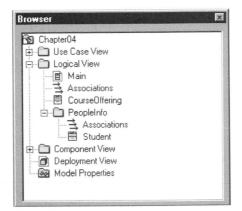

*Figure 4-9   Relocated Classes*

## OBJECTS AND CLASSES IN THE ESU COURSE REGISTRATION PROBLEM

WE WILL LOOK at the *Add a Course Offering to Teach* scenario, which is one of the subflows of the *Select Courses to Teach* use case. The main capability provided by this scenario is the ability for the professor to select a course offering to teach for a given semester.

Although we are looking at this process in a step-by-step manner, many of these steps may occur concurrently in the real world.

### Identify Boundary Classes

This use case interacts only with the Professor actor. The action specified in this scenario is only one capability provided by the use case (the use case also states that the Professor can modify a selection, delete a selection, review a selection, and print a selection). This means that something in the system must provide the ability for the Professor to select a capability. A class containing all the options available to the Professor as stated in the use case is created to satisfy this need. This class is called ProfessorCourseOptions. Additionally, we can identify a class that deals with the addition of a new Course Offering for the Professor. This class is called AddACourseOffering.

### Identify Entity Classes

This scenario deals with Courses, their Course Offerings, and the Professor assignment. We can identify three entity classes: Course, CourseOffering, and Professor.

### Identify Control Classes

We will add one control class to handle the flow of events for the use case. This class is called ProfessorCourseManager.

The identified classes (with stereotypes set to entity, control, or boundary) have been added to the model as shown in Figure 4-10. Since there is already an actor named Professor, Rational Rose will notify you that Professor now exists in multiple namespaces when you create the Professor class.

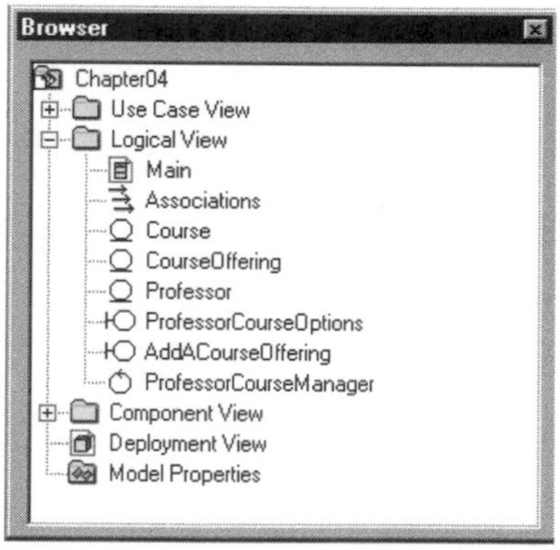

*Figure 4-10    Classes for the* **Add a Course Offering to Teach** *Scenario*

### Create Packages

The next step is to group classes into packages. At this time, we have identified six classes: Course, CourseOffering, Professor, Professor-CourseOptions, AddACourseOffering, and ProfessorCourseManager. They fall into three logical groups—things unique to the university, things that contain information about people, and things that are interfaces to actors. We can identify packages: Interfaces, University-Artifacts, and PeopleInfo. The classes are relocated to the identified packages. The packages along with their contained classes are shown in Figure 4-11.

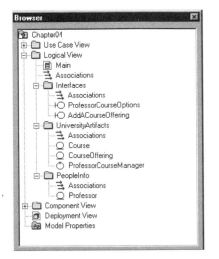

*Figure 4-11   Packages in the Browser*

## CLASS DIAGRAMS

AS MORE AND more classes are added to the model, a textual representation of the classes is not sufficient. Class diagrams are created to provide a picture or view of some or all of the classes in the model.

The main class diagram in the logical view of the model is typically a picture of the packages in the system. Each package also has its own main class diagram, which typically displays the "public" classes of the package. Other diagrams are created as needed. Some typical uses of other diagrams are the following:

- View of all the implementation classes in a package
- View of the structure and behavior of one or more classes
- View of an inheritance hierarchy

**THE MAIN CLASS DIAGRAM IN RATIONAL ROSE**

Rose automatically creates the Main class diagram in the Logical View of the model.

To add packages to the Main class diagram:

1. Double-click on the Main diagram in the browser to open the diagram.
2. Click to select the package in the browser.
3. Drag the package onto the diagram.
4. Repeat the preceding steps for each package that is to be added to the diagram.

The Main class diagram for the Registration System is shown in Figure 4-12.

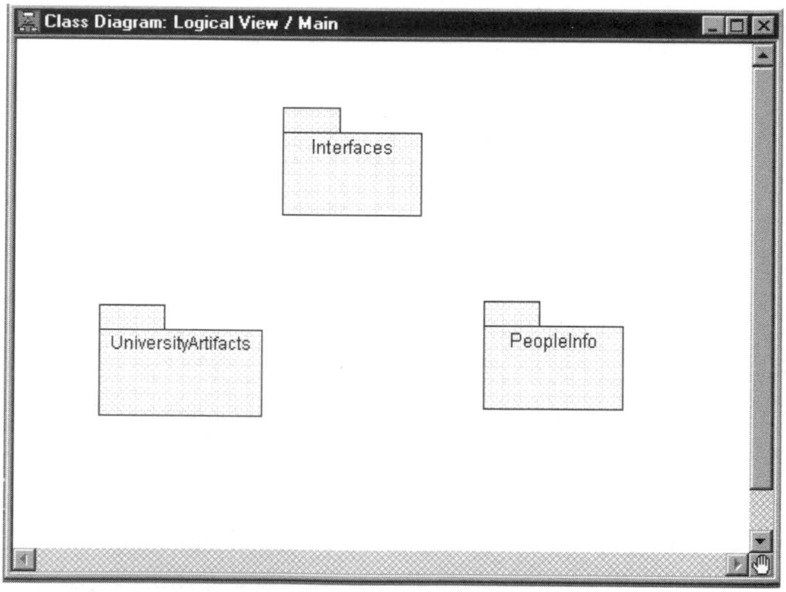

*Figure 4-12   Main Class Diagram*

**CREATING A PACKAGE MAIN CLASS DIAGRAM IN RATIONAL ROSE**

1. Double-click on the package on a class diagram.
2. Rose will "open" the package and create (or display) the main class diagram for the package.
3. Click to select a class in the browser and drag the class onto the diagram. (Note: The stereotype display of a class may be set using the Format: Stereotype display menu choice.)
4. Repeat step 3 for each additional class that is to be placed on the diagram.

The main class diagram for the UniversityArtifacts package is shown in Figure 4-13. Notice that the CourseOffering class is not on the diagram. This is an "implementation" class in the package and we decided not to show it on the main diagram of the package. As more packages and classes are added to the model, additional diagrams are created as needed.

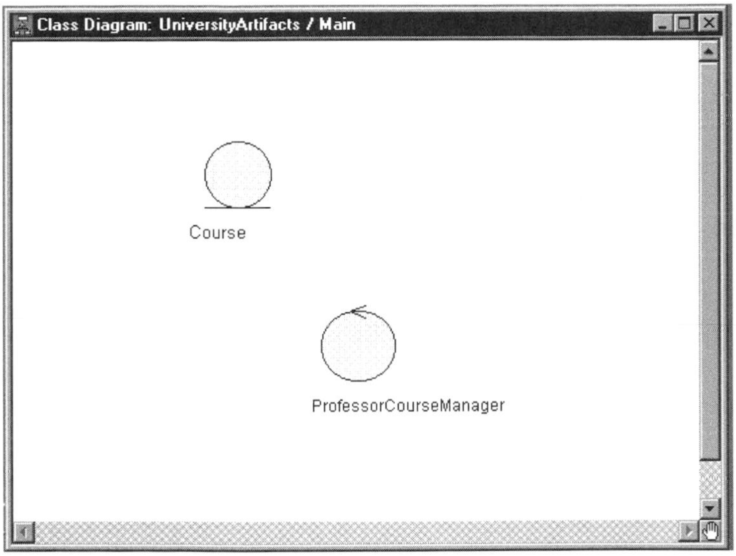

*Figure 4-13   UniversityArtifacts Package Main Class Diagram*

**TO SET VISIBILITY DISPLAY IN RATIONAL ROSE**

To set the default visibility display:

1.   Select the Tools:Options menu choice.
2.   Select the Diagram tab.
3.   Select the Show Visibility checkbox to set the default to show the visibility of all classes.

To set the visibility for a selected class:

1.   Right-click to select the class on a diagram and make the shortcut menu visible.
2.   Click to select or deselect the Options:Show Visibility menu choice.

A class diagram showing package visibility is shown in Figure 4-14.

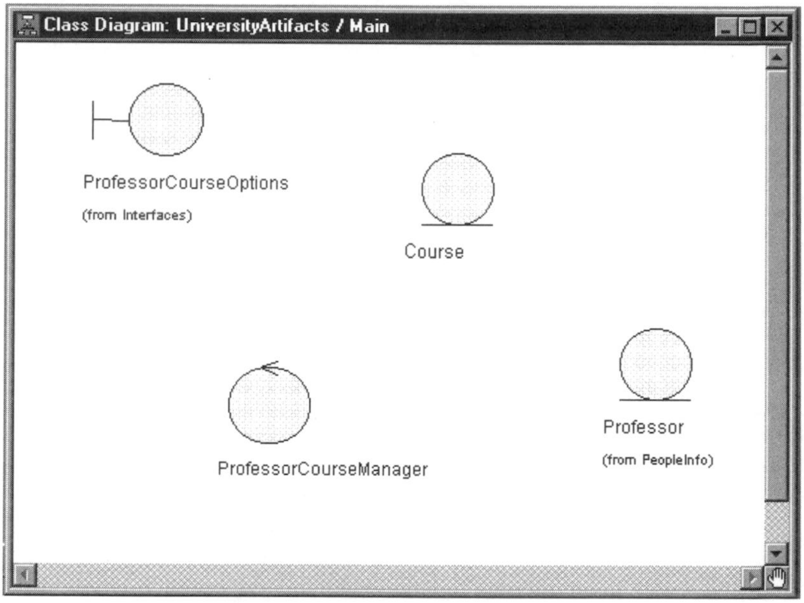

![Class Diagram: UniversityArtifacts / Main — showing ProfessorCourseOptions (from Interfaces), Course, ProfessorCourseManager, and Professor (from PeopleInfo)]

*Figure 4-14   Class Diagram with Package Visibility*

## SUMMARY

AN OBJECT IS a computer representation of an entity, either real world or invented. An object is a concept, abstraction, or thing with sharp boundaries and meaning for an application. Each object in a system has three characteristics: state, behavior, and identity. The state of an object is one of the possible conditions in which it may exist. Behavior determines how an object acts and reacts to requests from other objects. Identity states that each object is unique—even if its state is identical to that of another object.

A class is a description of a group of objects with common properties (attributes), common behavior (operations), common relationships to other objects (associations and aggregations), and common semantics. In the UML a class is drawn as a compartmented rectangle. The compartments show the class name, its structure, and its behavior. As classes are created, they should also be documented. The documentation should state the purpose of the class and not the structure of the class.

Stereotypes provide the capability to create a new type of modeling element. Stereotypes must be based on elements that are part of the UML metamodel. During analysis, three common stereotypes for a class are entity, boundary, and control. These stereotypes are useful in defining the classes needed for a system under development.

A package in the logical view of the model is a collection of related packages and/or classes. By grouping classes into packages, we can look at the "higher" level view of the model (i.e., the packages) or we can dig deeper into the model by looking at what is contained by the package.

Class diagrams are created to provide a picture or view of some or all of the classes in the model. Class diagrams may also be created in the use case view of the model. These diagrams typically are attached to use cases and contain a view of the classes participating in the use case.

## Chapter 5

# Discovering Object Interaction

## USE CASE REALIZATION

THE USE CASE diagram presents an outside view of the system. The functionality of the use case is captured in the flow of events. Scenarios are used to describe how use cases are realized as interactions among societies of objects. A scenario is an instance of a use case— it is one path through the flow of events for the use case. Scenarios are developed to help identify the objects, the classes, and the object interactions needed to carry out a piece of the functionality specified by the use case. Scenarios document decisions about how the responsibilities specified in the use cases are distributed among the objects and classes in the system. They also provide an excellent communication medium to be used in the discussion of the system requirements with customers. "Scenarios speak the language of the end user and the domain expert, and therefore provide a means for them to state their expectations about the desired behavior of a system to its developers."[1]

Each use case is a web of scenarios—primary scenarios (the normal flow for the use case) and secondary scenarios (the what-if logic of the use case). This means that there are numerous scenarios for any given system—all the primary and secondary scenarios for all the use cases. During the early stage of analysis it is safe to say that looking at the primary scenarios for each identified use case is enough. When you find that each new scenario is repeating a lot of steps from previously identified scenarios, then you have reached the finish line. "This phase of analysis should be drawn to a close once the team has elaborated approximately 80 percent of a system's primary scenarios along with a representative selection of the secondary ones. Elaborate upon any more, and your analysis will likely reach diminishing returns; elaborate upon any fewer, and you won't have a sufficient understanding of the desired behavior of the system to properly understand the risks."[2]

---

[1] Booch, Grady. *Object Solutions.* Redwood City, CA: Addison-Wesley, 1995.
[2] *Ibid.*

In the Rational Unified Process, use case realizations are captured in the Logical View of the model. We will again make use of the concept of a stereotype to show that the use cases that we create in the Logical View of our model are the realizations of the use cases contained in the Use Case View of our model. In other words, the use cases in the Logical View have the same name as the use cases in the Use Case View along with a stereotype of Realization. In the UML, use case realizations are drawn as dashed ovals as shown in Figure 5-1. These Logical View use cases typically are shown on a use case diagram (or set of use case diagrams) contained in the Logical View of your model.

Use Case Name

*Figure 5-1   UML Notation for a Use Case Realization*

**CREATING A LOGICAL VIEW USE CASE DIAGRAM IN RATIONAL ROSE**

1.  Right-click to select the Logical View package in the browser and make the shortcut menu visible.
2.  Select the New:Use Case Diagram menu choice. This will add a new use case diagram called NewDiagram to the browser.
3.  While the NewDiagram is still selected, enter the name Realizations.

A browser view of the Realizations Use Case Diagram is shown in Figure 5-2.

**CREATING USE CASE REALIZATIONS IN RATIONAL ROSE**

1.  Double-click on the Realizations use case diagram in the browser to open the diagram.
2.  Click to select the Use Case icon from the toolbar.
3.  Click on the use case diagram window to place the use case. This will place the new use case on the diagram and also add it to the browser.

4.  Double-click on the use case to open the Use Case Specification.

5.  Enter the name of the use case (same name as the use case in the Use Case View) in the Name field. (Note: You must enter the name in the Specification or in the Browser to invoke Rational Rose's namespace support. If you enter the name on the use case diagram, Rational Rose will assume that the use case is the same use case that is in the Use Case View.)

6.  Click the arrow in the Stereotype field to make the drop-down menu visible.

7.  Select use-case realization.

8.  Click the OK button to close the Use Case Specification.

The Realizations Use Case diagram is shown in Figure 5-3.

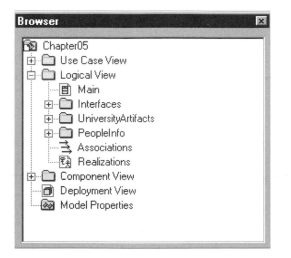

*Figure 5-2   Use Case Realization Diagram in the Browser*

Traceability between the use cases in the Logical View and the use cases in the Use Case View is visualized by adding the Use Case View use cases to the Realizations diagram and connecting them to their realizations using a realize relationship.

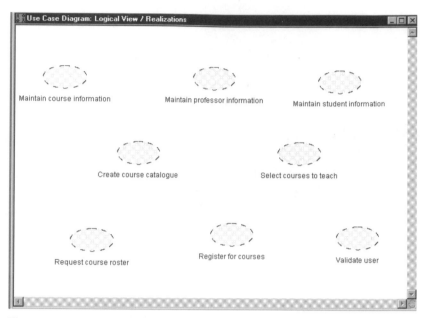

*Figure 5-3    Use Case Realization Diagram*

The Realizations Use Case diagram showing traceability is shown in Figure 5-4.

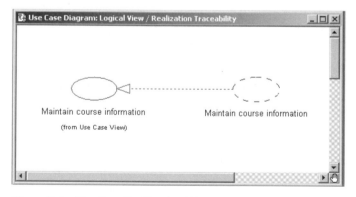

*Figure 5-4    Use Case Realization Diagram*

## DOCUMENTING SCENARIOS

THE FLOW OF events for a use case is captured in text, whereas scenarios are captured in interaction diagrams. There are two types of interaction diagrams—sequence diagrams and collaboration diagrams. Each diagram is a graphical view of the scenario.

## SEQUENCE DIAGRAMS

A SEQUENCE DIAGRAM shows object interactions arranged in time sequence. It depicts the objects and classes involved in the scenario and the sequence of messages exchanged between the objects needed to carry out the functionality of the scenario. Sequence diagrams typically are associated with use case realizations in the Logical View of the system under development.

In the UML, an object in a sequence diagram is drawn as a rectangle containing the name of the object, underlined. An object can be named in one of three ways: the object name, the object name and its class, or just the class name (anonymous object). The three ways of naming an object are shown in Figure 5-5.

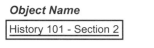

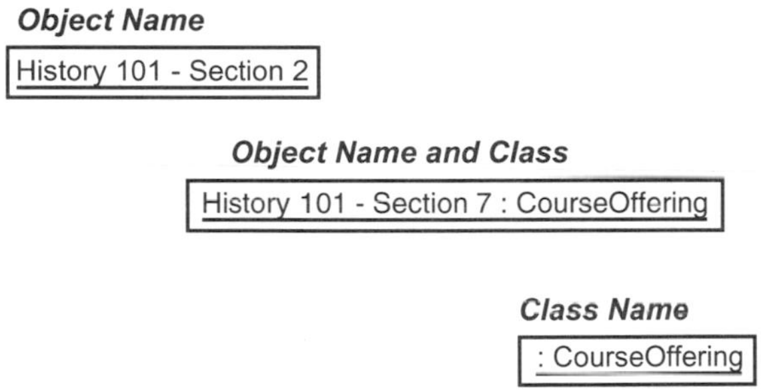

*Object Name*

| History 101 - Section 2 |

*Object Name and Class*

| History 101 - Section 7 : CourseOffering |

*Class Name*

| : CourseOffering |

*Figure 5-5   Naming Objects in a Sequence Diagram*

Object names can be specific (e.g., Algebra 101, Section 1) or they can be general (e.g., a course offering). Often, an anonymous object (class name only) may be used to represent any object in the class.

Each object also has its timeline represented by a dashed line below the object. Messages between objects are represented by arrows that point from the client (sender of the message) to the supplier (receiver of the message).

The UML notation for objects and messages in a sequence diagram is shown in Figure 5-6.

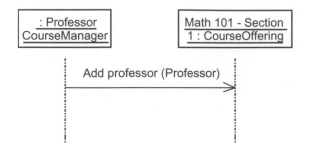

*Figure 5-6   UML Notation for Objects and Messages in a Sequence Diagram*

**CREATING A SEQUENCE DIAGRAM IN RATIONAL ROSE**

1. Right-click to select the use case realization in the Logical View of the browser and make the shortcut menu visible.
2. Select the New:Sequence Diagram menu choice. An unnamed sequence diagram is added to the browser.
3. With the new sequence diagram selected, enter the name of the sequence diagram.

The browser view of a sequence diagram is shown in Figure 5-7.

**CREATING OBJECTS AND MESSAGES IN SEQUENCE DIAGRAMS IN RATIONAL ROSE**

1. Double-click on the sequence diagram in the browser to open the diagram.
2. Click to select the actor in the browser.
3. Drag the actor onto the sequence diagram.
4. Click to select the Object icon from the toolbar.
5. Click on the sequence diagram window to place the object.
6. While the object is still selected, enter the name of the object.

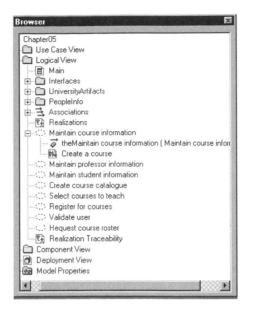

*Figure 5-7 Browser View of a Sequence Diagram*

7.  Repeat the preceding steps for each object and actor in the scenario.

8.  Click to select the Object Message icon from the toolbar.

9.  Click on the actor or object sending the message and drag the message line to the actor or object receiving the message.

10. While the message line is still selected, enter the name of the message.

11. Repeat steps 7 through 9 for each message in the scenario.

The sequence diagram for the *Create a Course* scenario is shown in Figure 5-8.

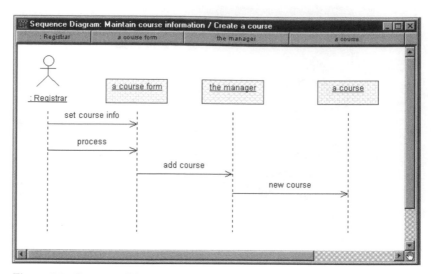

*Figure 5-8   Sequence Diagram*

**ASSIGNING OBJECTS IN A SEQUENCE
DIAGRAM TO CLASSES IN RATIONAL ROSE**

1.   Click to select the class in the browser.
2.   Drag the class onto the object in the sequence diagram.
     Rose will add the class name preceded by a colon (:) to the
     object name. If the object is unnamed, the name is set to
     :className. If the stereotype display for a class is set to
     icon, and if an icon exists, then the icon will be used in the
     sequence diagram.

A sequence diagram with the object "a course" assigned to the
Course class is shown in Figure 5-9.

## SEQUENCE DIAGRAMS
## AND BOUNDARY CLASSES

BOUNDARY CLASSES ARE added to sequence diagrams to show the
interaction with the user or another system. In the early analysis
phases, the purpose of showing boundary classes on a sequence diagram is to capture and document the interface requirements, *not*

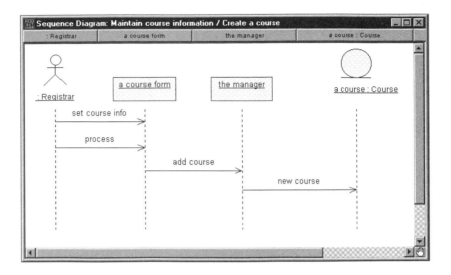

*Figure 5-9   Sequence Diagram with an Object Assigned to a Class*

to show how the interface will be implemented. The actual messages from the actor to the boundary class along with their sequencing information are dependent upon the application framework that is chosen later in development; thus they will probably change as more of the "how" is added to the system.

## COMPLEXITY AND SEQUENCE DIAGRAMS

EVERY TIME I teach a class, the question "How complex can a sequence diagram be?" is always asked. The answer I always give is "Keep them simple." The beauty of these diagrams is their simplicity—it is very easy to see the objects, the object interactions, the messages between the objects, and the functionality captured by the scenario.

The next question is usually "What do I do about conditional logic?" (all the *if, then, else* logic that exists in the real world). Here, you again have a very subjective answer. If the logic is simple, involving only a few messages, I usually add the logic to one diagram and use notes and scripts to communicate the choices to be made. On the other hand, if the *if, then, else* logic involves many complicated messages, I typically draw a separate diagram—one for the *if* case, one for the *then* case, and one for the *else* case. This is done to keep the diagrams simple. If you desire, diagrams may be linked to one another. This allows the user to navigate through a set of diagrams.

**LINKING DIAGRAMS IN RATIONAL ROSE**

1. Select the Note icon from the toolbar.
2. Click on the diagram to place the note.
3. Select the diagram that you wish to link in the browser and drag the diagram onto the note.
4. To navigate to the linked diagram, double-click on the note.

## COLLABORATION DIAGRAMS

A COLLABORATION DIAGRAM is an alternate way to show a scenario. This type of diagram shows object interactions organized around the objects and their links to each other. A collaboration diagram contains

- Objects drawn as rectangles
- Links between objects shown as lines connecting the linked objects
- Messages shown as text and an arrow that points from the client to the supplier

The UML notation for objects, links, and messages in a collaboration diagram is shown in Figure 5-10.

**CREATING COLLABORATION DIAGRAMS FROM SEQUENCE DIAGRAMS IN RATIONAL ROSE**

1. Double-click on the sequence diagram in the browser to open the diagram.
2. Choose the Browse:Create Collaboration Diagram menu choice or press the F5 key.
3. Rearrange the objects and messages on the diagram as needed.

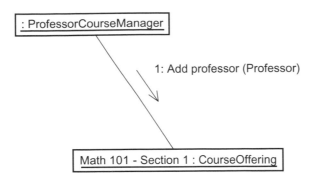

*Figure 5-10   UML Notation for Objects, Links, and Messages in a Collaboration Diagram*

The collaboration diagram is shown in Figure 5-11.

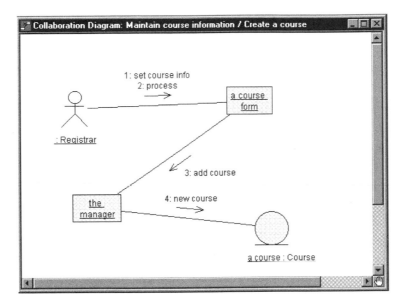

*Figure 5-11    Collaboration Diagram*

Collaboration diagrams can also be created from scratch. In that case, a sequence diagram can be created from the collaboration diagram by selecting the Browse:Create Sequence Diagram menu choice or by pressing the F5 key.

## WHY ARE THERE TWO DIFFERENT DIAGRAMS?

SEQUENCE DIAGRAMS PROVIDE a way to look at a scenario in a time-based order—what happens first, what happens next. Customers easily can read and understand this type of diagram. Hence, they are very useful in the early analysis phases. Collaboration diagrams tend to provide the big picture for a scenario since the collaborations are organized around the object links to one another. These diagrams seem to be used more in the design phase of development when you are designing the implementation of the relationships.

## SEQUENCE DIAGRAM FOR THE ESU COURSE REGISTRATION SYSTEM

CONTINUING WITH OUR analysis of the *Add a Course Offering* scenario, the diagram is shown in Figure 5-12.

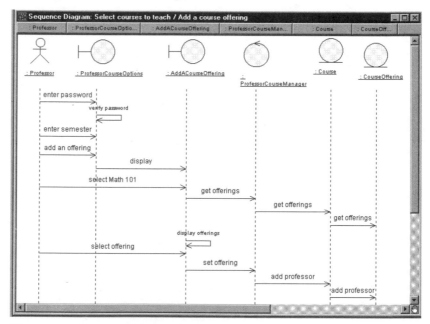

*Figure 5-12   Sequence Diagram for the* **Add a Course Offering** *Scenario*

Class diagrams may also be attached to use case realizations. These diagrams contain a view of the classes participating in the use case.

**CREATING A VIEW OF PARTICIPATING CLASSES IN RATIONAL ROSE**

1. Right-click on the use case realization in the browser to make the shortcut menu visible.
2. Select the New:Class Diagram menu choice.
3. While the diagram is still selected, enter the name of the class diagram.
4. Double-click on the diagram in the browser to open the diagram.
5. Click to select a class in the logical view of the browser and drag the class onto the diagram.
6. Repeat step 5 for each additional class that is to be placed onto the diagram.

The View of Participating Classes for the *Select Courses to Teach* use case is shown in Figure 5-13.

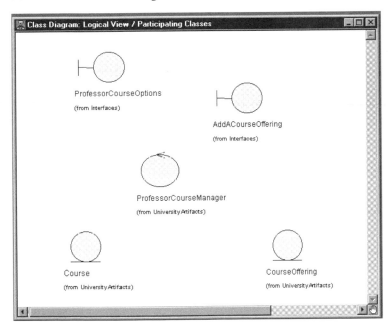

*Figure 5-13: View of Participating Classes*

## SUMMARY

THE USE CASE diagram presents an outside view of the system. The functionality of the use case is captured in the flow of events. Scenarios are used to describe how use cases are realized as interactions among societies of objects. A scenario is an instance of a use case— it is one path through the flow of events for the use case. Thus, each use case is a web of scenarios. Scenarios are developed to help identify the objects, the classes, and the object interactions needed to carry out a piece of the functionality specified by the use case.

The flow of events for a use case typically is captured in text, whereas scenarios are captured in interaction diagrams. There are two types of interaction diagrams—sequence diagrams and collaboration diagrams. Each diagram is a graphical view of the scenario.

A sequence diagram shows object interactions arranged in time sequence. A collaboration diagram is an alternate way to show a scenario. This type of diagram shows object interactions organized around the objects and their links to each other.

**Chapter 6**

# Specifying Relationships

## THE NEED FOR RELATIONSHIPS

ALL SYSTEMS ARE made up of many classes and objects. System behavior is achieved through the collaborations of the objects in the system. For example, a student is added to a course offering when the course offering receives the *add student* message. This is often referred to as an object sending a message to another object. Relationships provide the conduit for object interaction. Two types of relationships discovered during analysis are associations and aggregations.

## ASSOCIATION RELATIONSHIPS

AN ASSOCIATION IS a bidirectional semantic connection between classes. It is not a data flow as defined in structured analysis and design—data may flow in either direction across the association. An association between classes means that there is a link between objects in the associated classes. For example, an association between the Course class and the ProfessorCourseManager class means that objects in the Course class are connected to objects in the ProfessorCourseManager class. The number of objects connected depends upon the multiplicity of the association, which is discussed later in this chapter. In the UML, association relationships are shown as a line connecting the associated classes, as shown in Figure 6-1.

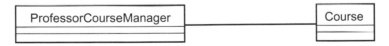

*Figure 6-1   UML Notation for an Association Relationship*

CREATING AN ASSOCIATION RELATIONSHIP IN RATIONAL ROSE

   1.   Click to select the Association icon from the toolbar. The association icon may be added to the toolbar by right-clicking on the toolbar and selecting the Customize menu command.

2.  Click on one of the associated classes in a class diagram.
3.  Drag the association line to the other associated class.

An association relationship is shown in Figure 6-2.

```
┌─────────────────────────────────────────────────────────────┐
│ ▣ Class Diagram: UniversityArtifacts / Main      _ □ ✕      │
├─────────────────────────────────────────────────────────────┤
│                                                              │
│          ┌───┐                                               │
│        ─┤│   │                                               │
│          └───┘                                               │
│                                                              │
│        ProfessorCourseOptions                                │
│                                                              │
│   (from Interfaces)                        ┌───┐             │
│                                           │     │            │
│                                            └───┘             │
│                                           ─────               │
│                                           Course             │
│                  ┌───┐  ◄────────────                        │
│                 │     │                                      │
│                  └───┘                                       │
│                                                              │
│         ProfessorCourseManager                               │
│                                                              │
└─────────────────────────────────────────────────────────────┘
```

*Figure 6-2     Association Relationship*


# AGGREGATION RELATIONSHIPS

AN AGGREGATION RELATIONSHIP is a specialized form of association in which a whole is related to its part(s). Aggregation is known as a "part-of" or containment relationship. The UML notation for an aggregation relationship is an association with a diamond next to the class denoting the aggregate (whole), as shown in Figure 6-3.

*Figure 6-3     UML Notation for an Aggregation Relationship*

The following tests may be used to determine if an association should be an aggregation:

- Is the phrase "part of" used to describe the relationship?
- Are some operations on the whole automatically applied to its parts? For example, delete a course then delete all of its course offerings.
- Is there an intrinsic asymmetry to the relationship where one class is subordinate to the other?

For example, a Course (Math 101) may be offered at different times during a semester. Each offering is represented as a Course Offering (e.g., Math 101, Section 1, and Math 101, Section 2). The relationship between a Course and a CourseOffering is modeled as an aggregation—a Course "has" CourseOfferings.

**CREATING AN AGGREGATION RELATIONSHIP IN RATIONAL ROSE**

1. Select the Aggregation icon from the toolbar. The Aggregation icon may be added to the toolbar by right-clicking on the toolbar and selecting the Customize menu command.
2. Click on the class playing the role of the "whole" in a class diagram and drag the aggregation line to the class playing the role of the "part."

An aggregation relationship is shown in Figure 6-4.

## ASSOCIATION OR AGGREGATION?

IF TWO CLASSES are tightly bound by a whole-part relationship, the relationship is typically an aggregation. "The decision to use aggregation is a matter of judgment and is often arbitrary. Often it is not obvious if an association should be modeled as an aggregation. If you exercise careful judgment and are consistent, the imprecise distinction between aggregation and ordinary association does not cause problems in practice."[1]

---

[1] Rumbaugh, James *et al. Object-Oriented Modeling and Design.* Upper Saddle River, NJ: Prentice Hall, 1991, p. 58.

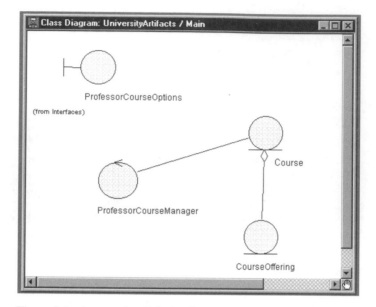

*Figure 6-4   Aggregation Relationship*

Whether a relationship is an association or an aggregation is often domain dependent. What type of relationship should be used to model a car with its tires? If the application is a service center, and the only reason you care about the tire is because it is part of the car you are servicing, then the relationship should be an aggregation. On the other hand, if the application is a tire store, you will care about the tire independent of a car and therefore, the relationship should be an association.

## NAMING RELATIONSHIPS

AN ASSOCIATION MAY be named. Usually the name is an active verb or verb phrase that communicates the meaning of the relationship. Since the verb phrase typically implies a reading direction, it is desirable to name the association so it reads correctly from left to right or top to bottom. The words may have to be changed to read the association in the other direction (e.g., a Professor *teaches* a Course, a Course *is taught by* a Professor). It is important to note that the name of the association is optional. Names are added if they are needed to add clarity to the model. Aggregation relationships typically are not named since they are read using the words "has" or "contains."

**NAMING RELATIONSHIPS IN RATIONAL ROSE**

1. Click to select the relationship line on a class diagram.
2. Enter the name of the relationship.

A named relationship is shown in Figure 6-5.

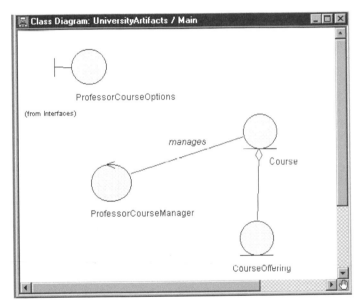

*Figure 6-5  A Named Association*

## ROLE NAMES

THE END OF an association where it connects to a class is called an association role. Role names can be used instead of association names. A role name is a noun that denotes the purpose or capacity wherein one class associates with another. The role name is placed on the association near the class that it modifies, and may be placed on one or both ends of an association line. It is not necessary to have both a role name and an association name.

CREATING ROLE NAMES IN RATIONAL ROSE

1.  Right-click on the relationship line near the class that it modifies to make the shortcut menu visible.
2.  Select the Role Name menu choice.
3.  Enter the name of the role.

Figure 6-6 shows an association with a role name.

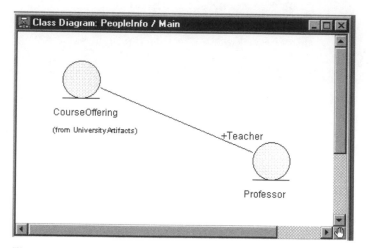

*Figure 6-6   Role Name*

The relationship shown in Figure 6-6 is read in both directions.

■  A Professor playing the role of the Teacher is related to the CourseOffering

■  A CourseOffering is related to a Professor playing the role of a Teacher

There is no standard as to whether you should use association names or role names. However, most people today tend to use role names instead of association names since it is easier to convey the meaning of the relationship. This is especially true in a bidirectional relationship since it is very hard to find a verb phrase that reads correctly in both directions. What verb phrase could be used to name the association in Figure 6-6? By using a role name, the meaning is clear in both directions.

Associations are named or role names are used only when the names are needed for clarity. If you have a relationship between Company and Person then you could use an association name called "employs" or the role names of "Employer" and "Employee" to convey an employment relationship. If the classes were named Employer and Employee, no name would be necessary since the meaning of the relationship is clear based on the names of the classes.

## MULTIPLICITY INDICATORS

ALTHOUGH MULTIPLICITY IS specified for classes, it defines the number of objects that participate in a relationship. Multiplicity defines the number of objects that are linked to one another. There are two multiplicity indicators for each association or aggregation—one at each end of the line. Some common multiplicity indicators are

| 1 | Exactly one |
|---|---|
| 0..* | Zero or more |
| 1..* | One or more |
| 0..1 | Zero or one |
| 5..8 | Specific range (5, 6, 7, or 8) |
| 4..7,9 | Combination (4, 5, 6, 7, or 9) |

**CREATING MULTIPLICITY IN RATIONAL ROSE**

1. Double-click on the relationship line to make the Specification visible.
2. Select the Detail tab for the role being modified (Role A Detail or Role B Detail).
3. Enter the desired multiplicity in the Cardinality field.
4. Click the OK button to close the Specification.

Multiplicity indicators are shown in Figure 6-7.

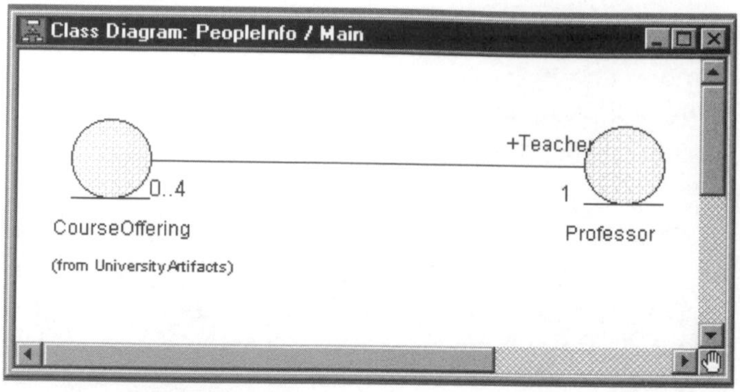

*Figure 6-7    Multiplicity Indicators*

The drawing in Figure 6-7 may be read in the following ways:

- One CourseOffering object is related to *exactly one* Professor object playing the role of the Teacher. For example, Math 101, Section 1 (a CourseOffering object) is related to Professor Smith (a Professor object).

- One Professor object playing the role of the Teacher is related to *zero to four* CourseOffering objects. For example, Professor Smith (a Professor object) is related to Math 101, Section 1; Algebra 200, Section 2; and Calculus 1, Section 3 (CourseOffering objects). Since the multiplicity is a range of zero to four, as few as zero CourseOffering objects to a maximum of four CourseOffering objects may be linked to one Professor object.

## REFLEXIVE RELATIONSHIPS

MULTIPLE OBJECTS BELONGING to the same class may have to communicate with one another. This is shown on the class diagram as a reflexive association or aggregation. Role names rather than association names typically are used for reflexive relationships.

**CREATING A REFLEXIVE RELATIONSHIP IN RATIONAL ROSE**

1. Select the Association (or Aggregation) icon from the toolbar.
2. Click on the class and drag the association (or aggregation) line outside the class.
3. Release the mouse button.
4. Click and drag the association (or aggregation) line back to the class.
5. Enter the role names and multiplicity for each end of the reflexive association (or aggregation).

A reflexive relationship is shown in Figure 6-8.

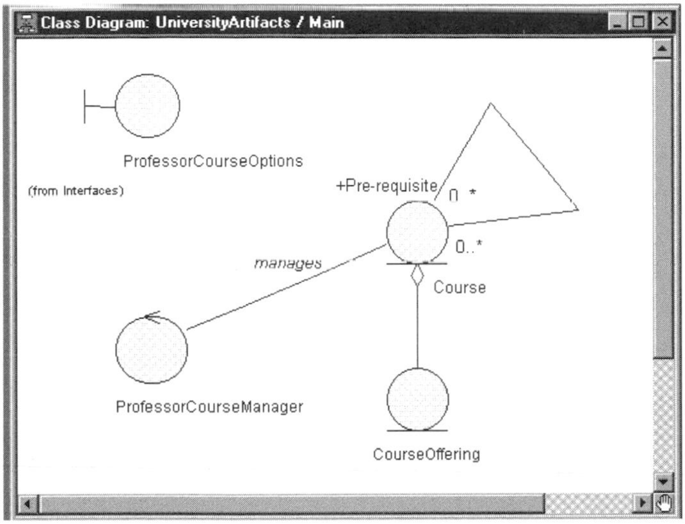

```
Class Diagram: UniversityArtifacts / Main            _ □ ✕

                    ○
       ┤○
         ProfessorCourseOptions
                                        +Pre-requisite  ⋂  *
     (from Interfaces)
                                              ○    0..*
            manages                            Course
              ○
         ProfessorCourseManager
                                         ○
                                     CourseOffering
```

*Figure 6-8   Reflexive Relationship*

The reflexive relationship in Figure 6-8 may be read in the following ways:

- One Course object playing the role of Prerequisite is related to zero or more Course objects.

- One Course object is related to zero or more Course objects playing the role of Prerequisite.

## FINDING RELATIONSHIPS

SCENARIOS ARE EXAMINED to determine if a relationship should exist between two classes. Messages between objects mean that the objects must communicate with each other. Associations and/or aggregations provide the pathway for communication.

Relationships may also be discovered based on the signature of an operation. This is discussed in Chapter 7.

### Relationships in the ESU Course Registration Problem

In the *Add a Course Offering* scenario, the communicating objects along with the relationship-type decisions that have been made are shown in Table 6-1.

| Sending Class | Receiving Class | Relationship Type |
|---|---|---|
| ProfessorCourseOptions | AddACourseOffering | Aggregation |
| AddACourseOffering | ProfessorCourseManager | Association |
| ProfessorCourseManager | Course | Association |
| Course | CourseOffering | Aggregation |

*Table 6-1   Class Relationships*

A class diagram with the added relationships is shown in Figure 6-9.

## PACKAGE RELATIONSHIPS

PACKAGE RELATIONSHIPS ARE also added to the model. The type of relationship is a dependency relationship, shown as a dashed arrow to the dependent package, as shown in Figure 6-10. If package A is dependent on package B this implies that one or more classes in package A initiates communication with one or more public classes in package B. Package A is referred to as the Client package and pack-

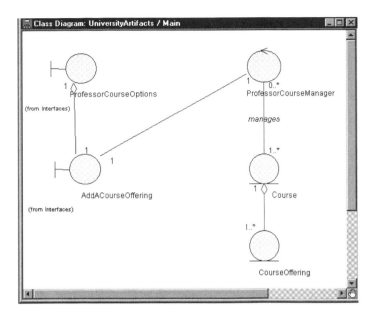

*Figure 6-9    Relationships in the* **Add a Course Offering** *Scenario*

age B is referred to as the Supplier package. Package relationships are also discovered by examining the scenarios and class relationships for the system under development. As this is an iterative process, the relationships will change as analysis and design progresses.

*Figure 6-10    Package Relationships*

## Package Relationships in the ESU Course Registration Problem

In the *Add a Course Offering* scenario, the AddACourseOffering class sends a message to the ProfessorCourseManager class. This implies that there is a relationship between the Interfaces package and the UniversityArtifacts package. At this time, we have not discovered any relationships to the People package.

**CREATING PACKAGE RELATIONSHIPS IN RATIONAL ROSE**

1.  Select the dependency relationship icon from the toolbar.
2.  Click on the client package and drag the arrow to the sup-plier package.

The package relationships for the Course Registration System are shown in Figure 6-11.

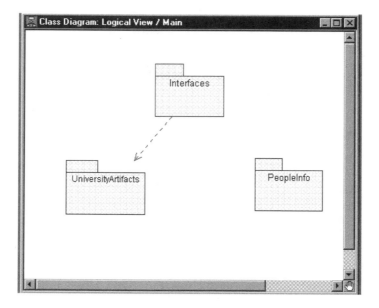

*Figure 6-11    Package Relationships in the ESU Course Registration System*

# SUMMARY

RELATIONSHIPS PROVIDE THE conduit for object interaction. Two types of relationships between classes that are discovered during analysis are associations and aggregations. An association is a bidirectional semantic connection between classes. An aggregation is a specialized form of association in which a whole is related to its part(s).

An association may be named. Usually the name is an active verb or verb phrase that communicates the meaning of the relationship. Roles can be used instead of association names. A role name is a noun that denotes the purpose or capacity wherein one class associates with another. Multiplicity is the number of instances that participate in a relationship. There are two multiplicity indicators for each association or aggregation—one at each end of the relationship line.

Multiple objects belonging to the same class may have to communicate with one another. This is shown on the class diagram as a reflexive association or aggregation.

Scenarios are examined to determine if a relationship should exist between two classes.

Packages are related via dependency relationships. If package A is dependent on package B, this implies that one or more classes in package A initiates communication with one or more public classes in package B.

Chapter 7

# Adding Behavior
# and Structure

# REPRESENTING BEHAVIOR AND STRUCTURE

A CLASS EMBODIES a set of responsibilities that define the behavior of the objects in the class. The responsibilities are carried out by the operations defined for the class. An operation should do only one thing and it should do it well! For example, a CourseOffering class needs to be able to add a student and remove a student. These responsibilities are represented by two operations—one that knows how to add a student and one that knows how to remove a student. All instances of the class will be able to perform the identified operations of the class.

The structure of an object is described by the attributes of the class. Each attribute is a data definition held by objects of the class. Objects defined for the class have a value for every attribute of the class. For example, a Course class has the attributes of name, definition, and number of credit hours. This implies that every Course object will have a value for each attribute. Attribute values do not have to be unique—there are many three-credit courses in the university.

As with classes, style guides should be followed while defining attributes and operations. In this case study, attributes and operations start with a lowercase letter, and underscores are not used—names composed of multiple words are pushed together and the first letter of each additional word is capitalized (e.g., numberOfStudents). Care should be taken to ensure that appropriate style guides are followed for all defined attributes and operations. This provides consistency across the classes, which leads to more readable and maintainable models and code.

If an object in a class does not need an attribute or operation, look at the class definition. This may be a sign that the class is not cohesive and should be broken up into separate classes. For example, suppose the CourseOffering class had the following attributes: offerNumber, location, timeOfDay, department, numberOfferingsInDepartment. A CourseOffering may care about its department but it probably does not care about the

number of other offerings in the department. A better model would
be a CourseOffering class related to a Department class. This is in
keeping with the general rule that a class should have a major theme.

## CREATING OPERATIONS

MESSAGES IN INTERACTION diagrams typically are mapped to operations of the receiving class. However, there are some special cases
where the message does not become an operation. If the receiving
class is a boundary class that is a placeholder for a graphical user
interface (GUI) type class, the message is a statement of the requirements for the GUI. These types of messages typically are implemented as some type of GUI control (i.e., a button) and are not
mapped to operations since the behavior is carried out by the GUI
control itself. For example, the Professor actor must enter a password
to start the *Add a Course Offering* scenario. This is represented as a
message to the boundary class ProfessorCourseOptions. This will
never be an operation of the user interface class—it will most likely
be a text field on a window. Messages to and from actors also receive
special consideration. If the message is to or from an actor that represents a physical person, the message is a statement of human pro-
cedure and is therefore incorporated into a user manual, but not to
an operation, since it does not make sense to create operations for
humans. In the *Add a Course Offering* scenario, the fact that the Professor must have some sort of password to activate the system is an
important requirement that should be captured in the user manual.
If the message is to or from an actor that represents an external system, a class is created to hold the protocol that is used to perform the
communication with the external system. In this case, the message
is mapped to an operation of the class.

Operations should be named in terms of the class performing
the operation, not the class asking for the functionality to be performed. For example, the operation to add a student to a course
offering is called *addStudent()*. Additionally, operation names should
not reflect the implementation of the operation since the implementation may change over time. For example, each CourseOffering
object has a maximum of ten students assigned to it. You may need

to ask the CourseOffering object how many students are assigned to it at a point in time. Today, the number is calculated by looking at the links from the CourseOffering object to Student objects. An operation called *calculateNumberOfStudents()* implies there is a calculation involved. Although this is the case today, it may not always be true (next year, the implementation may change to store the value in a file). A better name for the operation is *getNumberOfStudents()* since this does not imply how the operation is implemented.

**MAPPING MESSAGES TO NEW OPERATIONS IN RATIONAL ROSE**

1. Assign the objects to classes if that has not been done previously.
2. Right-click on the message arrow to make the shortcut menu visible.
3. Select the < new operation > menu choice. This will open the Operation Specification.
4. Enter the name of the operation in the Operation Specification.
5. Click the OK button to close the Operation Specification.

Note: If the desired operation already exists for the class, you do not have to re-create the operation; simply select the operation from the list of operations for the class.

A sequence diagram with operations is shown in Figure 7-1.

Operations may also be created independently of interaction diagrams, since not all scenarios are represented in a diagram. This is also true for operations that are created to "help" another operation. For example, a course might have to determine if a specified professor is certified to teach it before it adds the professor as the teacher. An operation called *validateProfessor()* could be an operation created to perform this behavior.

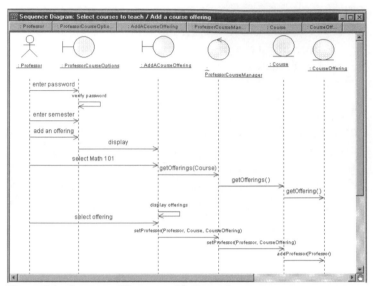

*Figure 7-1    Sequence Diagram with Operations*

CREATING OPERATIONS IN RATIONAL ROSE

1.  Right-click to select the class in the browser and make the pop-up menu visible.
2.  Select the New:Operation menu choice. This will create an operation called opname in the browser.
3.  With the new operation selected, enter the desired name.

Operations for the Course class are shown in Figure 7-2.

## DOCUMENTING OPERATIONS

EACH OPERATION SHOULD be documented so the reader of the model can quickly understand its purpose. The documentation should state the functionality performed by the operation. It should also state any input values needed by the operation along with the return value of the operation. The input and return values constitute the operation signature. This information may not be known initially. Instead, it may be added later in the life cycle when more is known about the class.

*Figure 7-2    Operations in the Browser*

**DOCUMENTING OPERATIONS IN RATIONAL ROSE**

1. Click the + next to the class in the browser to expand the class.
2. Click to select the operation.
3. Position the cursor in the documentation window and enter the documentation for the operation.

The documentation for the *setProfessor()* operation of the Course class is shown in Figure 7-3.

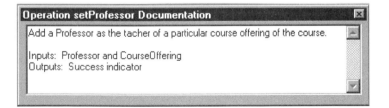

*Figure 7-3    Operation Documentation*

## RELATIONSHIPS AND OPERATION SIGNATURES

THE SIGNATURE OF an operation may indicate a relationship. If the class for an argument of an operation or the return from an operation is a fundamental class such as a String, the relationship typically is not shown on a diagram. For other classes (i.e., nonfundamental classes) the relationship typically is displayed on one or more class diagrams. For example, the two inputs to the setProfessor() operation of the Course class are professor (Professor class) and course offering (CourseOffering class). This implies that relationships exist between:

- Course and Professor
- Course and CourseOffering

Relationships based on operation signatures initially are modeled as associations that may be refined into dependency relationships as the design of the system matures. Refinement is covered in Chapter 12. Package relationships should also be reviewed as relationships based on operation signatures are added to the model. For example, we have now added a relationship between the Course class and the Professor class. This implies that there is a dependency relationship between the University Artifacts package and the People package.

## CREATING ATTRIBUTES

MANY OF THE attributes of a class are found in the problem statement, the set of system requirements, and the flow of events documentation. They may also be discovered when supplying the definition of a class. Finally, domain expertise is also a good source of attributes for a class. For example, the requirements state that information such as course name, description, and number of credit hours is available in the Course Catalog for a semester. This implies that name, description, and number of credit hours are attributes of the Course class.

**CREATING ATTRIBUTES IN RATIONAL ROSE**

1.  Right-click to select the class in the browser and make the pop-up menu visible.
2.  Select the New:Attribute menu choice. This will create an attribute called Name in the browser.
3.  With the new attribute selected, enter the desired name.

Attributes for the Course class are shown in Figure 7-4.

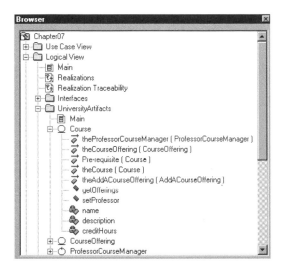

*Figure 7-4   Attributes in the Browser*

# DOCUMENTING ATTRIBUTES

ATTRIBUTES SHOULD ALSO be documented with a clear, concise definition. The definition should state the purpose of the attribute, not the structure of the attribute. For example, a bad definition for the name attribute of the Course class could be "a character string of length 15." A better definition for the name attribute is "The title of the course that is used in all University publications."

DOCUMENTING ATTRIBUTES IN RATIONAL ROSE

1.  Click the + next to the class in the browser to expand the class.
2.  Click to select the attribute.
3.  Position the cursor in the documentation window and enter the documentation for the attribute.

The documentation for the name attribute of the Course class is shown in Figure 7-5.

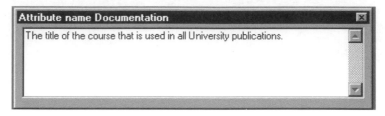

*Figure 7-5   Attribute Documentation*

# DISPLAYING ATTRIBUTES AND OPERATIONS

ATTRIBUTES AND OPERATIONS may be displayed on a class diagram. Often, a class diagram is created specifically for this purpose—it shows the structure and behavior of the classes in a package. Relationships typically are not shown on this diagram.

CREATING A CLASS DIAGRAM TO SHOW THE
ATTRIBUTES AND OPERATIONS FOR A PACKAGE

1.  Right-click to select the package in the browser and make the shortcut menu visible.
2.  Select the New:Class Diagram menu choice. A class diagram called NewDiagram will be added to the browser.
3.  With the new diagram selected, enter the name of the diagram.

### ADDING CLASSES TO A DIAGRAM USING THE QUERY MENU

1.  Double-click on the diagram in the browser to open the diagram.
2.  Select the Query:Add Classes menu choice.
3.  Select the desired package.
4.  Click to select the desired classes and click the > > > > button to add the classes to the diagram or click the All > > button to add all the classes to the diagram.

### FILTERING RELATIONSHIPS IN RATIONAL ROSE

1.  Double-click on the diagram in the browser to open the diagram.
2.  Select the Query:Filter Relationships menu choice.
3.  Click the None button in the Type field to hide all relationships shown on the open diagram.
4.  Click the OK button to close the Relations window.

### DISPLAYING SOME ATTRIBUTES OR OPERATIONS IN RATIONAL ROSE

1.  Right-click to select the class on an open class diagram and make the shortcut menu visible.
2.  Select the Options:Select Compartment Items menu choice.
3.  Click to select the attributes and operations to be displayed.
4.  Click the > > > > button.
5.  Click the OK button to close the Edit Compartment window.

### SHOWING ALL ATTRIBUTES AND OPERATIONS IN RATIONAL ROSE

1.  Right-click on the class in a diagram to make the shortcut menu visible.
2.  Select the Options:Show All Attributes menu choice to display all the attributes for the class.
3.  Repeat step 1 and select the Options:Show All Operations menu choice to display all the operations for the class.

Note: To always display the attributes and operations for a class, you can set the Show All Attributes and Show All Operations selections using the Tools:Options menu.

**SETTING STEREOTYPE DISPLAY IN RATIONAL ROSE**

1. Right-click on the class in a diagram to make the shortcut menu visible.
2. Select the desired Options:Stereotype Display menu choice (None = do not display stereotype, Label = show stereotype in < < > >, Icon = show class using Stereotype icon).

The class diagram called Attributes and Operations for the University Artifacts package is shown in Figure 7-6. For this type of diagram I prefer to show the stereotypes of the classes as labels.

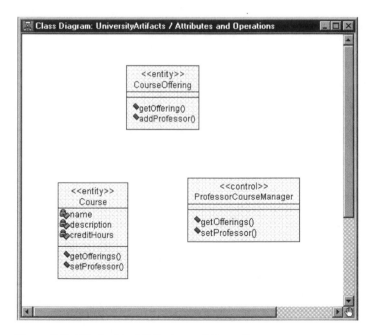

*Figure 7-6   Displaying Attributes and Operations*

## ASSOCIATION CLASSES

A RELATIONSHIP MAY also have structure and behavior. This is true when the information deals with a link between two objects and not with one object by itself.

Consider the following example: A student may take up to four course offerings, and course offering may have between three and ten students. Each student must receive a grade for the course offering. Where is the grade held? It doesn't belong to the student since a student will probably have different grades for different course offerings, and it doesn't belong to the course offering since a course offering has different grades for different students. The information belongs to the link between a student and a course offering. This is modeled as an association class. Since an association class behaves like any other class, it too can have relationships. Following our example, a student receives a report card each semester that is made up of all the linked grade objects for the student.

**CREATING ASSOCIATION CLASSES IN RATIONAL ROSE**
1. Click to select the Class icon from the toolbar.
2. Click on the diagram to place the class.
3. With the class selected, enter the name of the class.
4. Add the attributes and operations to the class.
5. Click to select the Association Class icon from the toolbar.
6. Click on the association class and drag the association class line to the association it modifies.
7. Create any additional relationships for the association class.

The association class Grade is shown in Figure 7-7.

## SUMMARY

A CLASS EMBODIES a set of responsibilities that define the behavior of the objects in the class. The responsibilities are carried out by the operations defined for the class. The structure of an object is

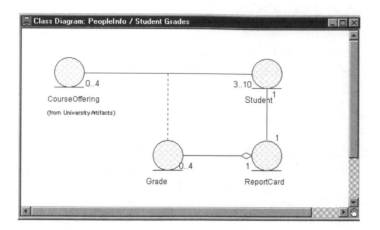

*Figure 7-7   Association Class*

described by the attributes of the class. Each attribute is a data definition held by objects of the class. Objects defined for the class have
a value for every attribute of the class. The attributes and operations
defined for a class are the ones that have meaning and utility within
the application that is being developed.

Messages in interaction diagrams typically are mapped to operations of the receiving class. However, there are some special cases
where the message does not become an operation: messages to and
from actors representing people and messages to and from classes
representing GUI classes.

Many of the attributes of a class are found in the problem statement, the set of system requirements, and the flow of events documentation. They may also be discovered when supplying the
definition of a class. Finally, domain expertise is also a good source
of attributes for a class.

A relationship may also have structure and behavior. This is
true when the information deals with a link between two objects
and not with one object by itself. The structure and behavior
belonging to a relationships is held in an association class.

Chapter 8

# Discovering Inheritance

# INHERITANCE

INHERITANCE DEFINES A relationship among classes where one class shares the structure and/or behavior of one or more classes. A hierarchy of abstractions is created in which a subclass inherits from one or more superclasses. Inheritance is also called an "is-a" or "kind-of" hierarchy. A subclass will inherit all attributes, operations, and relationships defined in any of its superclasses. Thus, attributes and operations are defined at the highest level in the hierarchy at which they are applicable, which allows all lower classes in the hierarchy to inherit them. Subclasses may be augmented with additional attributes and operations that apply only to that level of the hierarchy. A subclass may supply its own implementation of an operation. Since an inheritance relationship is not a relationship between different objects, the relationship is never named, role names are not used, and multiplicity does not apply.

There is no limit to the number of classes allowed in an inheritance hierarchy. However, practical experience has shown that typical C++ class hierarchies contain between three and five layers, whereas Smalltalk applications may be a bit deeper.

Inheritance is the key to reuse. A class can be created for one application and then a subclass may be created to add more information needed for a different application.

There are two ways to find inheritance—generalization and specialization. Both methods typically are used for any system under development.

# GENERALIZATION

GENERALIZATION PROVIDES THE capability to create superclasses that encapsulate structure and behavior common to several classes. This is very common in beginning analysis endeavors since the classes that currently exist are those that model the real world. Classes are examined for commonality of structure (attributes) and behavior (operations). For example, the Student and Professor classes both have name, address, and phoneNumber as attributes.

You should be on the lookout for synonyms since attribute and operation names are expressed in natural language and the commonality might be hidden. Additionally, look at attributes and behavior, which at first glance may seem specific, but in reality may be generalized. For example, the Student class has an attribute called studentID and the Professor class has an attribute called professorID. A general attribute called userID could be created to replace the studentID and the professorID as long as the individual IDs follow the same numbering scheme (e.g., they are both four-digit numbers). If they are different (e.g., the studentID is a ten-digit alphanumeric and the professorID is a four-digit number) then they should be kept separate.

## SPECIALIZATION

SPECIALIZATION PROVIDES THE ability to create subclasses that represent refinements to the superclass—typically, structure and behavior are added to the new subclass. This method of finding inheritance often comes into play if a class already exists. Subclasses are added to specialize the behavior of an existing class. For example, the registration system could be expanded to allow senior citizens to take classes free of charge. A new subclass called SeniorCitizen could be added to the RegistrationUser hierarchy to hold information pertinent to senior citizens.

Operations may be overridden by a subclass. However, a subclass should never restrict an operation defined in its superclasses. That is, the subclass should never provide less behavior or structure than its superclasses.

**CREATING INHERITANCE IN RATIONAL ROSE**

1. Open the class diagram that will display the inheritance hierarchy.
2. Click to select the Class icon from the toolbar and click on the open class diagram to draw the class.
3. With the class still selected, enter the name of the class. Note: The class could also be created in the browser and added to the open class diagram.
4. Click to select the Generalization icon on the toolbar.
5. Click on a subclass and drag the generalization line to the superclass.
6. Repeat step 5 for each additional subclass.

An inheritance relationship is shown in Figure 8-1.

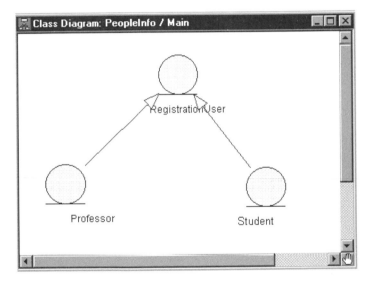

*Figure 8-1   Inheritance Relationship*

## INHERITANCE TREES

THE BASIS FOR specialization (i.e., why subclasses were created) in an inheritance relationship is called the *discriminator.* The discriminator typically has a finite set of values and subclasses that may be created for each value. For example, one basis for discrimination for a Course class is the location of the course—OnCampusCourse and OffSiteCourse could be two subclasses of the Course class based on this discriminator. The inheritance relationship may be shown as a tree for all subclasses created from one discriminator. Another subclass of Course could be MandatoryCourse. This subclass would not be part of the inheritance tree because it belongs to a different discriminator—course type. Care must be taken when you discover multiple discriminators for a class—for example, what happens when a mandatory course is held on campus. Do you have a multiple inheritance situation? Should aggregation be used? As analysis and design progresses, the answers to these questions will lead to the structure of the model.

**CREATING AN INHERITANCE TREE IN RATIONAL ROSE**

1. Open the class diagram that will display the inheritance hierarchy.
2. Click to select the Class icon from the toolbar and click on the open class diagram to draw the class.
3. With the class still selected, enter the name of the class. Note: The class could also be created in the browser and added to the open class diagram.
4. Click to select the Generalization icon on the toolbar.
5. Click on one subclass and drag the generalization line to the superclass.
6. For each subclass that is part of the inheritance tree, select the Generalization icon from the toolbar, click on the subclass, and drag the generalization line to the inheritance triangle.

Note: An inheritance tree may be created from two separate generalization arrows by selecting one arrow and dragging it onto the other arrow.

An inheritance tree relationship is shown in Figure 8-2.

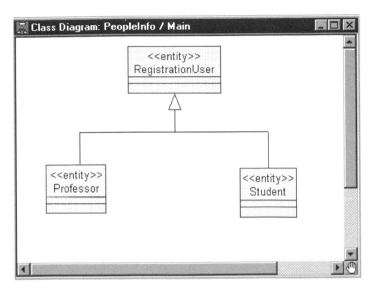

*Figure 8-2   Inheritance Tree*

I also like to show stereotypes as labels in this type of diagram since the inheritance triangle may obscure the class name if an icon is used.

Attributes, operations, and relationships are relocated to the highest applicable level in the hierarchy once a superclass is created. What features should be relocated? Let's look at the RegistrationUser hierarchy. The attributes, operations, and relationships for the subclasses are shown in Figure 8-3. As long as name and IDNumber have the same format they may safely be moved to the superclass (RegistrationUser). Both classes have a relationship to the CourseOffering class. There are two options that may be chosen for this relationship:

- Keep the relationships at the subclass level.

- Have one relationship at the superclass level with a multiplicity that includes the professor and the student objects (i.e., one CourseOffering object would be related to 4–11 RegistrationUser objects). Here a constraint stating that one RegistrationUser object must be a Professor object should be added to the model.

Which way is correct? They both are. Which way is the best to use? It depends. If you have a need for a CourseOffering object to know all the students and the professor, then having one list containing this information might be handy. This would imply that the second option is the way to go. If, on the other hand, you need to know only students or professors but not both at the same time, then the first option is probably best. It all comes down to what the system needs to do! This will be discovered by carefully examining the use cases and scenarios to discover the needed behavior.

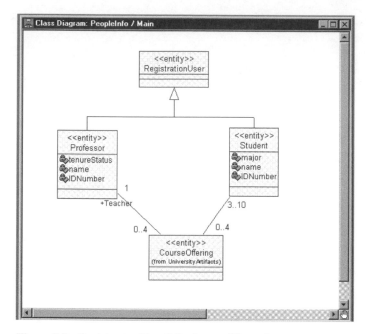

*Figure 8-3    RegistrationUser Inheritance Hierarchy*

**RELOCATING ATTRIBUTES AND OPERATIONS IN RATIONAL ROSE**

1.  Click the + sign next to one subclass in the browser to expand the class.
2.  Select the attribute or operation to be relocated.
3.  Drag the attribute or operation to the superclass.
4.  Delete the attribute or operation from all other subclasses.
5.  Repeat steps 2 through 4 for each additional attribute or operation to be relocated.

Relocated attributes are shown in Figure 8-4.

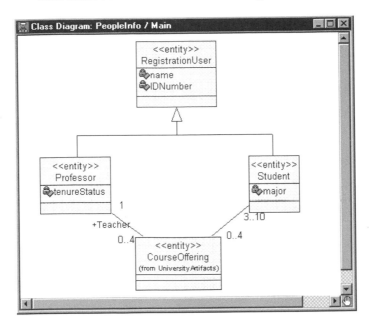

*Figure 8-4   Relocated Attributes and Operations*

# SINGLE INHERITANCE
# VERSUS MULTIPLE INHERITANCE

WITH SINGLE INHERITANCE, a class has one set of parents—that is, there is one chain of superclasses (e.g., a car is a motor vehicle, which is a vehicle). Multiple inheritance involves more than one chain of superclasses (e.g., an amphibious vehicle is a motor vehicle, which is a vehicle, and an amphibious vehicle is a water vehicle, which is a vehicle). There can be numerous problems associated with multiple inheritance—for example, name clashes and multiple copies of inherited features. How the problems are overcome is very language dependent from the use of special features of C++ (e.g., virtual base classes) to lack of support for multiple inheritance altogether (PowerBuilder). Multiple inheritance also leads to less maintainable code—the more superclasses, the harder it is to determine what comes from where and what happens if I change something.

The bottom line: Use multiple inheritance only when it is needed and always use it with care!

## INHERITANCE VERSUS AGGREGATION

INHERITANCE IS OFTEN misused—the "inheritance is good, therefore, the more I use the better my code will be" syndrome. This is not true—in fact, the misuse of inheritance can lead to problems. For example, a student may be full time or part time. A Student super-class with two subclasses—FulltimeStudent and ParttimeStudent—could be created. Multiple problems can arise with this structure. What happens if:

- A full-time student decides to go to school only part time? This implies that an object would have to change its class.

- Another dimension is added (e.g., on scholarship or not on scholarship)? Here you would have to add additional subclasses to model the scholarship information along with multiple inheritance to handle all the combinations (full-time student on scholarship, part-time student on scholarship, etc.).

Inheritance should be used to separate commonality from specifics. Aggregation should be used to show composite relationships. Often the two types of relationships are used together. The Student class has a classification (aggregation) that is either Fulltime or Parttime (inheritance). This is shown in Figure 8-5.

## SUMMARY

INHERITANCE PROVIDES THE capability to create a hierarchy of classes where common structure and behavior are shared among classes. The term superclass is the name given to the class holding the common information. The descendants are called subclasses. A subclass inherits all attributes, operations, and relationships that are defined

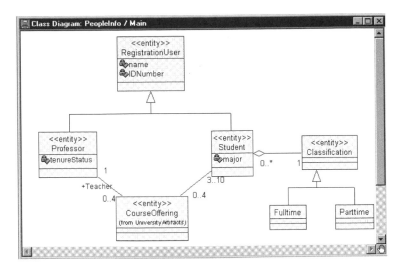

*Figure 8-5   Inheritance versus Aggregation*

for all of its superclasses. There are two ways to find inheritance in any system: generalization and specialization. Generalization provides the ability to create superclasses to encapsulate structure and/or behavior common to several classes. Specialization provides the capability to create subclasses that represent refinements or additions to the structure and/or behavior specified in the superclass.

# Chapter 9

# Analyzing Object Behavior

# MODELING DYNAMIC BEHAVIOR

USE CASES AND scenarios provide a way to describe system behavior; that is, the interaction between objects in the system. Sometimes it is necessary to look at the behavior inside an object. A statechart diagram shows the states of a single object, the events or messages that cause a transition from one state to another, and the actions that result from a state change.

A statechart diagram will not be created for every class in the system, only for classes with "significant" dynamic behavior. Interaction diagrams can be studied to determine the dynamic objects in the system—ones receiving and sending many messages. Statechart diagrams are also useful to investigate the behavior of an aggregate "whole" class and of control classes.

Care must be taken to stay in an analysis frame of mind—concentrating on the WHAT of the problem and not the HOW of the solution.

**CREATING STATECHART DIAGRAMS IN RATIONAL ROSE**

1.  Right-click to select the class in the browser and make the shortcut menu visible.
2.  Select the New:Statechart Diagram menu choice. This will add a state diagram called NewDiagram to the browser.
3.  While the diagram is still selected, enter the name of the diagram.
4.  To open the diagram, click the + to expand the class in the browser, click the + to expand the State/Activity Model in the browser and double-click on the statechartdiagram in the browser.

The browser view of the statechart diagram for the CourseOffering class is shown in Figure 9-1.

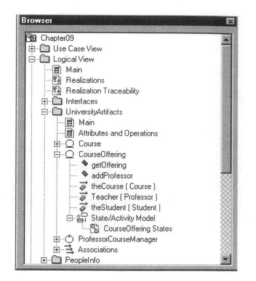

*Figure 9-1   Statechart Diagram in the Browser*

## STATES

A STATE IS a condition during the life of an object during which it satisfies some condition, performs some action, or waits for an event. The state of an object may be characterized by the value of one or more of the attributes of the class. For example, a CourseOffering object may be open (able to add a student) or closed (maximum number of students already assigned to the CourseOffering object). The state depends upon the number of students assigned to the particular CourseOffering object. Additionally, a state of an object may be characterized by the existence of a link to another object. A professor may be teaching or on sabbatical. This depends upon the existence of a link to a CourseOffering object. Looking at the state of an object can validate the multiplicity chosen for a relationship to another object. That is, if being in a state depends upon the existence of a link to another object, this implies that the multiplicity of the relationship modifying the role of the associated class must include zero (i.e., the relationship is optional). Thus, the states of an object are found by examining the attributes and links defined for the object.

The UML notation for a state is a rectangle with rounded corners as shown in Figure 9-2.

*Figure 9-2   UML Notation for a State*

A statechart diagram encompasses all the messages that an object can send and receive. Scenarios represent one path through a statechart diagram. The interval between two messages sent by an object typically represents a state. Therefore, sequence diagrams may be examined to discover the states for an object (look at the space between the lines representing messages received by the object). If we had created sequence diagrams for each use case in the ESU Course Registration system, we would discover that objects in CourseOffering class can be in one of the following states: Initialization (created prior to registration but students have not been added to it), Open (able to accept students), Closed (maximum number of students already registered for it), Canceled (no longer offered).

**CREATING STATES IN RATIONAL ROSE**

1.  Click to select the State icon from the toolbar.
2.  Click to place the state on the statechart diagram.
3.  With the state still selected, enter the name of the state.

The states of the CourseOffering class are shown in Figure 9-3.

## STATE TRANSITIONS

A STATE TRANSITION represents a change from an originating state to a successor state (which may be the same as the originating state). An action can accompany a state transition.

There are two ways to transition out of a state—automatic and nonautomatic. An automatic state transition occurs when the activity of the originating state completes—there is no named event associated with the state transition. A nonautomatic state transition is

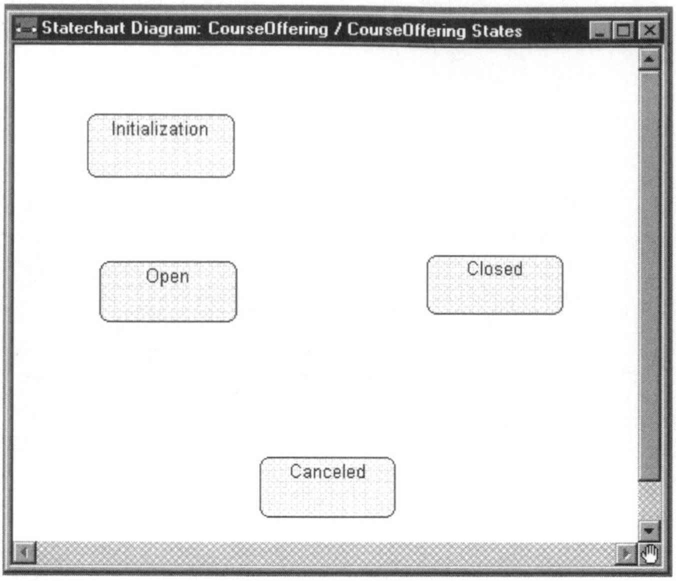

Statechart Diagram: CourseOffering / CourseOffering States

Initialization

Open

Closed

Canceled

*Figure 9-3   States*

caused by a named event (either from another object or from outside the system). Both types of state transitions are considered to take zero time and cannot be interrupted. A state transition is represented by an arrow that points from the originating state to the successor state.

**CREATING STATE TRANSITIONS IN RATIONAL ROSE**

1.   Click to select the State Transition icon from the toolbar.
2.   Click to select the originating state on the statechart diagram.
3.   Drag the state transition to the successor state.
4.   If the state transition is a named transition, enter the name while the state transition arrow is still selected.

State transitions are shown in Figure 9-4.

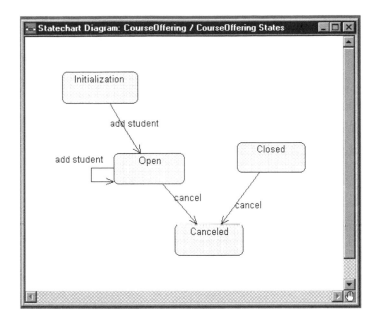

*Figure 9-4   State Transitions*

## SPECIAL STATES

THERE ARE TWO special states that are added to the statechart diagram. The first is a start state. Each diagram must have one and only one start state since the object must be in a consistent state when it is created. The UML notation for a start state is a small solid-filled circle as shown in Figure 9-5. The second special state is a stop state. An object can have multiple stop states. The UML notation for a stop state is a bull's eye, as shown in Figure 9-5.

*Start State*                    *Stop State*

*Figure 9-5   UML Notation for Start and Stop States*

**CREATING START STATES IN RATIONAL ROSE**

1. Click to select the Start icon from the toolbar.
2. Click on the statechart diagram to draw the Start icon.
3. Click to select the State Transition icon from the toolbar.
4. Click on the Start icon and drag the arrow to the desired state.

A start state is shown in Figure 9-6.

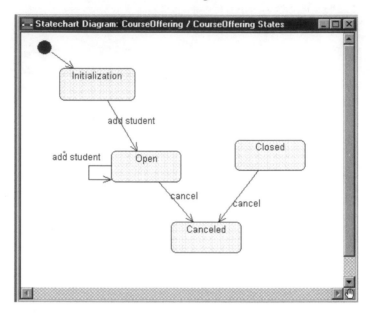

*Figure 9-6    Start State*

**CREATING STOP STATES IN RATIONAL ROSE**

1. Select the Stop icon from the toolbar.
2. Click on the statechart diagram to draw the Stop icon.
3. Select the State Transition icon from the bar.
4. Click on the state and drag the arrow to the Stop icon.

A stop state is shown in Figure 9-7.

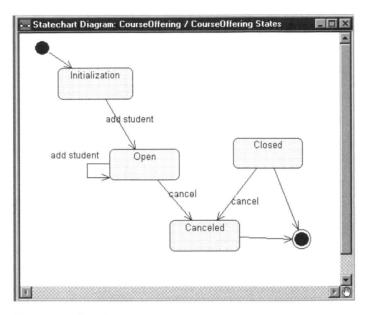

*Figure 9-7   Stop State*

## STATE TRANSITION DETAILS

A STATE TRANSITION may have an action and/or a guard condition associated with it and may also trigger an event. An action is behavior that occurs when the state transition occurs. An event is a message that is sent to another object in the system. A guard condition is a Boolean expression of attribute values that allows a state transition only if the condition is true. Both actions and guards are behaviors of the object and typically become operations. Often, these operations are private—that is, they are used only by the object itself. The UML notation for state transition detailed information is shown in Figure 9-8.

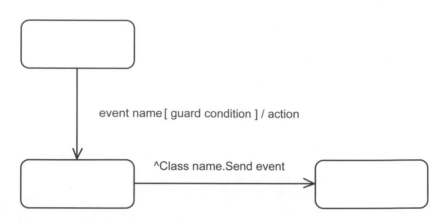

*Figure 9-8   UML Notation for State Transition Details*

**ADDING STATE TRANSITION DETAILS IN RATIONAL ROSE**

1.  Right-click on the state transition arrow to make the short-cut menu visible.
2.  Select the Open Specification menu choice.
3.  Select the Detail tab.
4.  Enter the action, guard, and/or the event to be sent.
5.  Click the OK button to close the specification.

State transition detail is shown in Figure 9-9.

## STATE DETAILS

ACTIONS THAT ACCOMPANY all state transitions into a state may be placed as an entry action within the state. Likewise, actions that accompany all state transitions out of a state may be placed as exit actions within the state. Behavior that occurs within the state is called an activity. An activity starts when the state is entered and either completes or is interrupted by an outgoing state transition. The behavior may be a simple action or it may be an event sent to

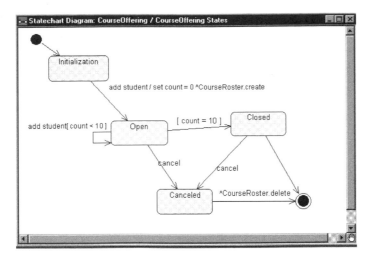

*Figure 9-9    State Transition Details*

another object. As with actions and guards, this behavior typically is mapped to operations on the object. The UML notation for state detailed information is shown in Figure 9-10.

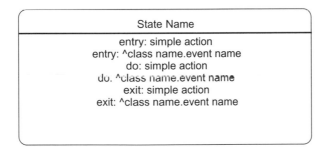

*Figure 9-10    State Details*

**CREATING ENTRY ACTIONS, EXIT ACTIONS,
AND ACTIVITIES IN RATIONAL ROSE**

1.  Right-click on the state to make the shortcut menu visible.
2.  Select the Open Specification menu choice.
3.  Select the Actions tab.
4.  Right-click in the Action field to make the shortcut menu visible.
5.  Select the Insert menu choice. This will create an action called entry.
6.  Double-click on entry to make the Action Specification visible.
7.  Select when the action should occur: on entry, on exit, do, or on event.
8.  Enter the action or event information.
9.  Select the type: action or send event.
10. Enter the action name and event information (if needed).
11. Click the OK button to close the Action Specification.
12. Click the OK button to close the State Specification.

A state with detailed information is shown in Figure 9-11.

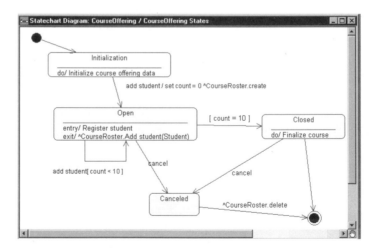

*Figure 9-11    State Details*

# SUMMARY

CLASSES THAT EXHIBIT "significant" dynamic behavior are analyzed further by creating statechart diagrams. This type of diagram shows all the states of an object, the events that the object receives, and the resulting actions that are taken. State transition events along with their accompanying actions are considered to take zero time and cannot be interrupted. States, along with their accompanying activities, can be interrupted.

# Chapter 10

# Checking the Model

## WHY HOMOGENIZE?

ACCORDING TO *Webster's New Collegiate Dictionary,* the word *homogenize* means to blend into a smooth mixture, to make homogeneous. As more use cases and scenarios are developed it is necessary to make the model homogeneous. This is especially true if multiple teams are working on different parts of the model. Since use cases and scenarios deal with the written word, people may use different words to mean the same thing or they may interpret words differently. At this time classes may be combined, classes may be split into multiple classes, or a class may be eliminated from the model. This is just the natural maturation of the model during the project life cycle.

Homogenization does not happen at one point in the life cycle—it *must* be on-going. Projects that wait until the end to synch up information developed by multiple groups of people are doomed to failure. I have found that the most successful projects are made up of teams that have constant communication mechanisms employed. Communication may be as simple as a phone call or as formal as a scheduled meeting—it all depends on the project and the nature of the need to talk (for example, is it a simple question or a formal review of a piece of the system?). The only thing that matters is the fact that the teams are not working in isolation.

## COMBINING CLASSES

IF DIFFERENT TEAMS are working on different scenarios, a class may be called by different names. The name conflicts must be resolved. This is accomplished mainly through model walk-throughs. Examine each class along with its definition. Also examine the attributes and operations defined for the classes, and look for the use of synonyms. Once you determine that two classes are doing the same thing, choose the class with the name that is closest to the language used by the customers.

Pay careful attention to the control classes created for the system. Initially, one control class is allocated per use case. This might be overkill—control classes with similar behavior may be combined. Examine the sequencing logic in the control classes for the system. If it is very similar, the control classes may be combined into one control class.

In the ESU Course Registration System there is a control class for the *Maintain Course Information* use case and one for the *Create Course Catalog* use case. Each control class gets information from a boundary class and deals with course information. It is possible that these two control classes could be combined since they have similar behavior and access similar information.

## SPLITTING CLASSES

CLASSES SHOULD BE examined to determine if they are following the golden rule of OO, which states that a class should do one thing and do it really well. They should be cohesive; for example, a StudentInformation class that contains information about the Student actor as well as information about what courses the student has successfully completed is doing too much. This is better modeled as two classes—StudentInformation and Transcript, with an association between them.

Often, what appears to be only an attribute ends up having structure and behavior unto itself and should be split off into its own class. For example, we'll look at Departments in the university. Each Course is sponsored by a Department. Initially, this information was modeled as an attribute of the Course class. Further analysis showed that it was necessary to capture the number of students taking classes in each department, the number of professors that teach department courses, and the number of courses offered by each department. Hence, a Department class was created. The initial attribute of Department for a Course was replaced with an association between Course and Department.

## ELIMINATING CLASSES

A CLASS MAY be eliminated altogether from the model. This happens when:

- The class does not have any structure or behavior
- The class does not participate in any use cases

In particular, examine control classes. Lack of sequencing responsibility may lead to the deletion of the control class. This is especially true if the control class is only a pass-through—that is, the control class receives information from a boundary class and immediately passes it to an entity class without the need for sequencing logic.

In the ESU Course Registration System, initially we would create a control class for the *Select Courses to Teach* use case. This use case provides the capability for professors to state what course offerings they will teach in a given semester. There is no sequencing logic needed for the control class—the professor enters the information on the GUI screen and the Professor is added to the selected offering. Here is a case where the control class for the use case could be eliminated.

## CONSISTENCY CHECKING

CONSISTENCY CHECKING IS needed since the static view of the system, as shown in class diagrams, and the dynamic view of the system, as shown in use case diagrams and interaction diagrams, are under development in parallel. Because both views are under development concurrently they must be cross-checked to ensure that different assumptions or decisions are not being made in different views.

Consistency checking does not occur during a separate phase or a single step of the analysis process. It should be integrated throughout the life cycle of the system under development.

Consistency checking is best accomplished by forming a small team (five to six people at most) to do the work. The team should be composed of a cross-section of personnel—analysts and designers, customers or customer representatives, domain experts, and test personnel.

## SCENARIO WALK-THROUGH

A PRIMARY METHOD of consistency checking is to walk through the high-risk scenarios as represented by a sequence or collaboration diagram. Since each message represents behavior of the receiving class, verify that each message is captured as an operation on the class diagram. Verify that two interacting objects have a pathway for communication via either an association or an aggregation. Especially check for reflexive relationships that may be needed since these relationships are easy to miss during analysis. Reflexive relationships are needed when multiple objects of the same class interact during a scenario.

For each class represented on the class diagram, make sure the class participates in at least one scenario. For each operation listed for a class, verify that either the operation is used in at least one scenario or it is needed for completeness. Finally, verify that each object included in a sequence or collaboration diagram belongs to a class on the class diagram.

## EVENT TRACING

FOR EVERY MESSAGE shown in a sequence or collaboration diagram, verify that an operation on the sending class is responsible for sending the event and an operation on the receiving class expects the event and handles it. Verify that there is an association or aggregation on the class diagram between the sending and receiving classes. Add the relationship to the class diagram if it is missing. Finally, if a state transition diagram for the class exists, verify that the event is represented on the diagram for the receiving class. This is needed because the diagram shows all the events that a class may receive.

## DOCUMENTATION REVIEW

EACH CLASS SHOULD be documented! Check for uniqueness of class names and review all definitions for completeness. Ensure that all attributes and operations have a complete definition. Finally, check that all standards, format specifications, and content rules established for the project have been followed.

## SUMMARY

AS MORE USE cases and scenarios are developed it is necessary to make the model homogeneous. This is especially true if multiple teams are working on different parts of the model. Classes are examined to determine if:

- Two or more classes may be combined
- One class should be split
- A class should be eliminated altogether

Consistency checking must be performed throughout the life cycle of any project. Consistency checking is needed because several views of the system are under development in parallel and care must be taken to ensure that the models stay in synch. There are three ways to perform consistency checking: scenario walk-throughs, event tracing, and review of the model documentation.

# Chapter 11

# Designing the
# System Architecture

# THE NEED FOR ARCHITECTURE

OVER THE YEARS I have heard many definitions of software architecture that range from "software architecture is what software architects do" to "software architecture is politics." I have come to the conclusion that software architecture is very difficult to define. It is a range of artifacts that are used to specify the strategic decisions about the structure and behavior of the system, the collaborations among the system elements, and the physical deployment of the system.

"Establishing a sound architectural foundation is absolutely essential to the success of an object-oriented project. Some teams try to ignore this phase, either because they are in such a rush to get a product out quickly they feel they don't have time to architect, or because they don't believe that architecting gives them any real value. Either way, the resulting head-long rush to code is always disastrous: fail to carry out this step properly, and your project will likely experience software meltdown."[1]

Architecture development is a very complicated issue. The architecture of the system is developed iteratively in the elaboration phase of development. "The architecture of a proposed system does not appear in a flash. It takes exploration of the use cases, a proof-of-concept prototype, an architectural baseline, and other efforts during the Inception and Elaboration phases."[2] Executable prototypes of the architecture are built to verify that the design decisions are correct. "Building something executable is absolutely essential, because it forces the development team to validate their design assumptions in the harsh light of reality."[3]

---

[1] Booch, Grady. *Object Solutions.* Redwood City, CA: Addison-Wesley, 1995.
[2] Jacobson, Ivar. *The Objector Software Development Process.* Draft edition.
[3] *Ibid.*

## THE ARCHITECTURE TEAM

EACH PROJECT SHOULD have a chief architect who may be assisted by a small team of people. "The main activities of the architect include the definition of the architecture of the software, the maintenance of the architectural integrity of the software, the assessment of the technical risks of the project, the definition of the order and content of the successive iterations along with the planning of each iteration, providing consulting to various design, implementation, integration, and quality assurance teams and assisting in providing future market directions."[4]

## THE 4 + 1 VIEW OF ARCHITECTURE

SOFTWARE ARCHITECTURE IS not a one-dimensional thing—it is made up of concurrent multiple views. Figure 11-1 shows the different views of software architecture.[5] The rest of this chapter addresses the elements in each view of the architecture along with the UML notation used to represent the architectural decisions made for the system.

## THE LOGICAL VIEW

THIS VIEW OF architecture addresses the functional requirements of the system—what the system should provide in terms of services to its users. The logical architecture is captured in class diagrams that contain the classes and relationships that represent the key abstractions of the system under development. Most of the UML notation that has been addressed so far is contained within this view of architecture (e.g., classes, associations, aggregations, generalization, and packages).

---

[4] Kruchten, Philippe. *Software Architecture and Iterative Development*. Santa Clara, CA: Rational Software Corporation, April 1994. p. 53.
[5] *Ibid.*

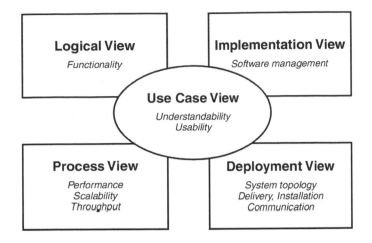

*Figure 11-1   The 4 + 1 View of Architecture*

This view of architecture is addressed early in the elaboration phase with the creation of classes and packages that represent the major abstractions of the domain. As time moves on, more classes and packages are added to the model to reflect the decisions made concerning the key mechanisms of the system. A key mechanism is a decision regarding common standards, polices, and practices. The selection of the key mechanisms for a system is often referred to as tactical design. "Poor tactical design can ruin even the most profound architecture, and so the team must mitigate this risk by explicitly identifying the project's key policies."[6] Some common key mechanisms involve the selection of an implementation language, persistent data storage, the look and feel of the user interface, error handling, communication mechanisms, object distribution and object migration, and networking.

Today, many patterns exist that may be used to implement the key mechanism decisions made for your system. I strongly recommend looking into patterns before you try to "roll your own."

---

[6] Booch, Grady. *Object Solutions.* Redwood City, CA: Addison-Wesley, 1995.

Additionally, the concepts of cohesion, closure, and reuse will affect the choices that you make. Robert Martin discusses some of the ramifications of the choice of packages for your system in his book *Designing Object-Oriented C++ Applications Using the Booch Method.* Although this book uses the Booch notation and process, it is still applicable to the Rational Unified Process and the UML. The bottom line is this: The UML may be used to communicate the strategic decisions made for your system by adding packages and classes to the model to communicate, implement, and document these decisions.

### Sample Key Mechanisms for the ESU Course Registration Problem

Since most of the development team had prior experience using the C++ language and because this system eventually will be expanded to include other university functionality, C++ is the language of choice by the architecture team. The architecture team also decided that a particular set of graphical user interface (GUI) controls should be used to control the look and feel of the user interface, and therefore, a package called GUI Controls is added to the model. The database persistence strategy chosen by the architecture team is the use of a corresponding database class (shadow class) for each persistent class in the system. Although other strategies that mainly involve the use of inheritance could have been chosen by the team, this strategy was chosen due to the fact that expertise in implementing this method of persistence already existed and the team felt that it had the least amount of risk. A database package containing the shadow classes is added to the model at this time. Additionally, it was decided to make use of the C++ features of catch and throw for exceptions. Rather than have each class be responsible for knowing how to catch and throw exceptions, a package called Error Handling is added to the model. Finally, a set of commercial foundation classes was chosen for this system. The packages representing the key mechanism decisions made for the course registration system are shown in Figure 11-2.

Since the Error Handling package and the Foundations package are used by every other package in the system, they are global packages.

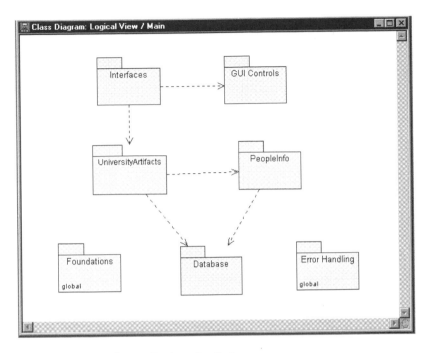

*Figure 11-2   ESU Course Registration System*

**MAKING A PACKAGE GLOBAL IN RATIONAL ROSE**

1. Right-click to select the package on a class diagram.
2. Select the Open Specification menu choice.
3. Select the Detail tab.
4. Click to select the global checkbox.
5. Click the OK button to close the specification.

## THE IMPLEMENTATION VIEW

THIS VIEW OF architecture concerns itself with the actual software module organization within the development environment. The implementation view of architecture takes into account derived requirements related to ease of development, software management, reuse, and constraints imposed by programming languages and development tools. The modeling elements in the component view of architecture are packages and components along with their connections.

A package in this view of architecture represents a physical partitioning of the system. The packages are organized in a hierarchy of layers where each layer has a well-defined interface. The fact that an object-oriented system tends to be a layered system should not bring any surprises. This is due to the definition of an object—it should do one thing and do it well! A drawing showing some typical layers of a system may be found in Figure 11-3.

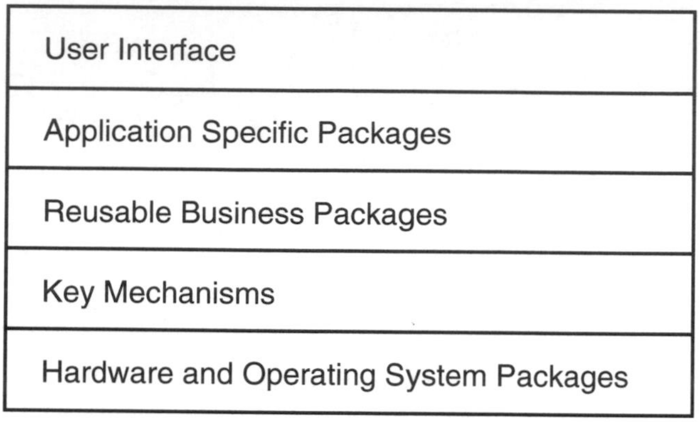

| User Interface |
| Application Specific Packages |
| Reusable Business Packages |
| Key Mechanisms |
| Hardware and Operating System Packages |

*Figure 11-3   System Layers*

The UML notation for a package in the component view is the same as a package in the logical view—a notched folder as found in Figure 11-4.

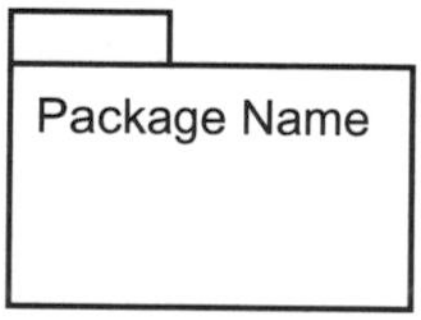

Package Name

*Figure 11-4   UML Notation for a Package*

**CREATING COMPONENT VIEW PACKAGES IN RATIONAL ROSE**

1.  Right-click to select the Component View package on the browser and make the shortcut menu visible.
2.  Select the New:Package menu choice. This will add an item called NewPackage to the browser.
3.  With the NewPackage still selected, enter the name of the package.

The main component diagram typically is a view of the packages defined for the system.

**THE MAIN COMPONENT DIAGRAM IN RATIONAL ROSE**

1.  Double-click on the Main Diagram under the Component View package on the browser to open the diagram.
2.  Click to select a package and drag the package onto the diagram.
3.  Repeat step 2 for each additional package.
4.  Dependency relationships are added by selecting the Dependency icon from the toolbar, clicking on the package representing the client, and dragging the arrow to the package representing the supplier.

The main component diagram for the ESU Course Registration problem is shown in Figure 11-5.

### Source Code Components

In the Component View of the model, a source code component represents a software file that is contained by a package. The type of file is language dependent (e.g., in C++, software components represent .h and .cpp files, in Java they represent .java files, and in Power-Builder a software component is a .pbl). Each component is assigned a language that is discussed in the language-dependent appendixes. Classes in the Logical View are mapped to components in the Component view. In C++, the mapping is typically one-to-one; that is, one class maps to one component. However, there are times that

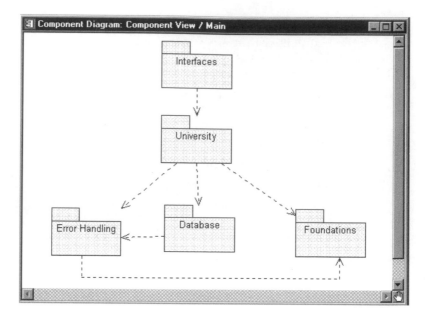

*Figure 11-5   Main Component Diagram*

more that one class will be mapped to a component. This is usually done when there is very tight coupling between the classes. For example, a container and its iterator are contained within one .h and one .cpp file. In this case, the container and the iterator classes would be mapped to one component. I have also seen classes that represent a pattern of collaboration mapped to one physical file. The UML notation for a component is shown in Figure 11-6.

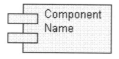

*Figure 11-6   UML Notation for a Component*

## Software Components in the
## ESU Course Registration Problem

This is a relatively simple system and the decision was made to provide a one-to-one mapping between classes and components—each class has its own header and .cpp file.

**CREATING COMPONENTS IN RATIONAL ROSE**

1. Open a component diagram.
2. Click to select the Component icon on the toolbar.
3. Click on the diagram to place the component. This will also add the component to the Browser.
4. While the component is still selected, enter the name of the component.

A sample component diagram is shown in Figure 11-7.

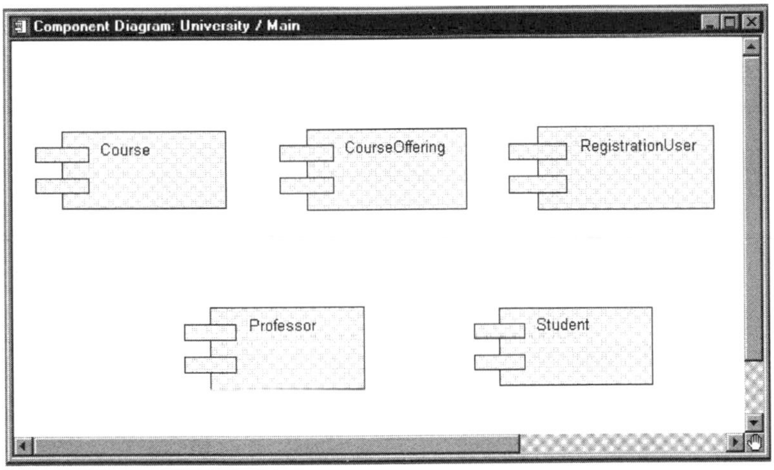

*Figure 11-7   Software Components*

**MAPPING CLASSES TO COMPONENTS IN RATIONAL ROSE**

1. Right-click to select the component on the browser and make the shortcut menu visible.
2. Select the Open Specification menu choice.
3. Select the Realizes tab.
4. Right-click to select the class and make the shortcut menu visible.
5. Select the Assign menu choice.
6. Click the OK button to close the Specification.

Note: A class may also be assigned to a component by selecting it in the browser and dragging it onto the component (in the browser or on a component diagram).

The Component Specification for the CourseOffering component is shown in Figure 11-8.

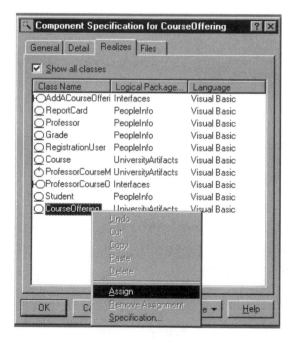

*Figure 11-8    Component Specification for the CourseOffering component*

## THE PROCESS VIEW

THIS VIEW OF architecture focuses on the run-time implementation structure of the system. The process view of architecture takes into account requirements such as performance, reliability, scalability, integrity, system management, and synchronization. Components are also used in this view of architecture. Component diagrams are created to view the run-time and executable components created for the system. Components are related via dependency relationships. Run-time components show the mapping of classes to run-time libraries such as Java applets, Active-X components, and dynamic libraries. Executable components show the interfaces and calling dependencies among executables. Stereotypes may be used to visualize the type of component. Interface classes that are created during design are shown using lollypop notation as shown in Figure 11-9.

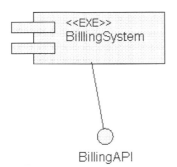

*Figure 11-9　Component Interface*

In Rational Rose, the information for the process view of architecture is created as diagrams in the Component View of the tool containing either run-time or executable components. Diagrams are created to show dependencies between the different types of components in the system.

For the ESU Course Registration System, the architecture team decided that there would be two DLLs—one containing course and course offering information and one containing database information. This allocation was chosen since it was felt that the course structure and the choice of database strategy was subject to change. By making them libraries, only the libraries would have to be replaced to implement future changes. There are three executables for the system—one for the Registrar to create and maintain the system, one for the Student to access the system, and one for the Professor to access the system. There is no communication between the executables. The component diagram for the Professor executable (ProfessorOptions.exe) is shown in Figure 11-10.

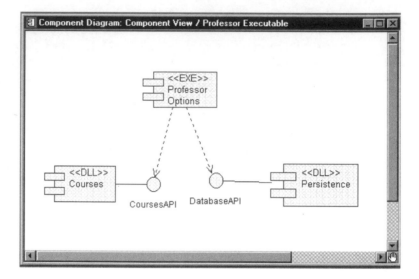

*Figure 11-10   Professor Executable*

## THE DEPLOYMENT VIEW

THIS VIEW OF architecture involves mapping software to processing nodes—it shows the configuration of run-time processing elements and the software processes living on them. The deployment view takes into account requirements such as system availability, reliability, performance, and scalability. Deployment diagrams are created to show the different nodes along with their connections in the system. The deployment diagram visualizes the distribution of components across the enterprise. Run-time processing elements are represented as nodes, which are connected by associations indicating communication paths between them. Software processes are illustrated as text attached to a node or group of nodes.

This diagram allows the architecture team to understand the system topology and aids in mapping components to executable processes. Issues such as processor architecture, speed, and capacity, along with interprocess communication bandwidth/capacity, physical location of the hardware, and distributed processing techniques, all come into play.

### Deployment Diagram for the ESU Course Registration System

After studying the component packages defined for the problem, examining existing hardware, and estimating the load on the system during the course registration period, the architecture team decided that they will need five processors for the system—one to handle the professor executable, one for the database, and three for student registration.

**CREATING THE DEPLOYMENT DIAGRAM IN RATIONAL ROSE**

1. Rose automatically creates the deployment diagram. To open the diagram, double-click on the Deployment Diagram on the browser.
2. To create a node, click to select the Processor icon and click on the diagram to place the node.
3. With the node still selected, enter the name of the node.
4. To create a connection between nodes, click to select the Connection icon from the tool bar, click on one node on the deployment diagram, and drag the connection to the other node.

The deployment diagram for the ESU Course Registration problem is shown in Figure 11-11.

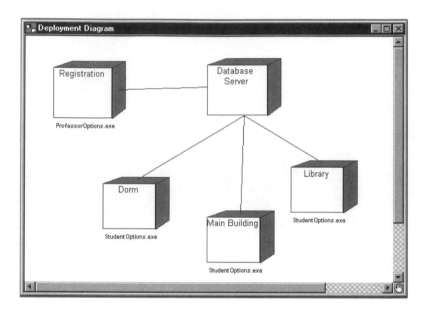

*Figure 11-11   Deployment Diagram*

## THE USE CASE VIEW

THIS VIEW OF architecture demonstrates and validates the logical, process, component, and deployment views. Sequence diagrams and collaboration diagrams are created to show how the various design elements interact to produce the desired behavior.

## SUMMARY

SOFTWARE ARCHITECTURE IS not one-dimensional—it is made up of concurrent multiple views: logical, implementation, process, and deployment. Scenarios are developed to validate the four different views. Good architectures are constructed in well-defined layers of abstraction where there is a clear separation between the interface and implementation of each layer. Key mechanisms focus on decisions regarding common standards, policies, and practices. Packages are created to show the architectural layout of the system. Architecture also addresses the physical layout of the system. Component diagrams are created to show components that are the physical implementation of the system. Deployment diagrams are created to show the hardware configuration that is used for the system under development.

# Chapter 12

# Building the Iterations

## THE ITERATION PLANNING PROCESS

THE ITERATION RELEASE plan prescribes schedules for all the increments of the system. "Such a plan must identify a controlled series of architectural releases, each growing in its functionality and ultimately encompassing the requirements of the complete production system."[1]

"The iteration plan must state the iteration specific goals:

- Capabilities being developed

- Risks being mitigated during this iteration

- Defects being fixed during the iteration

Exit criteria:

- Updated capability information

- Updated risk mitigation plan

- A release description document, which captures the results of an iteration

- Test cases and results of the tests conducted on the products including a list of defects

- An iteration plan, detailing the next iteration including measurable evaluation criteria for assessing the results of the next iteration(s)"[2]

The scenarios developed during analysis are the main input to this phase of development. The scenarios are examined and prioritized according to risk, importance to the customer, and the need to develop certain basic scenarios first. This task is best accomplished with a team made up of a domain expert, analysts, the architect, and testing personnel. "Scenarios should be grouped so that for each release, they collectively provide a meaningful chunk of the

---

[1] Booch, Grady. *Object Solutions.* Redwood City, CA: Addison-Wesley, 1995.

[2] Kruchten, Philippe. *A Rational Development Process.* Rational Software Corporation. Available at www.rational.com.

system's behavior and additionally require the development team to attack the project's next highest risks."[3] As each iteration is completed, risks are reevaluated and the project plan is updated as needed. "For most projects, plan on about five (plus or minus two) intermediate releases."[4]

The iteration planning process is shown in Figure 12-1.

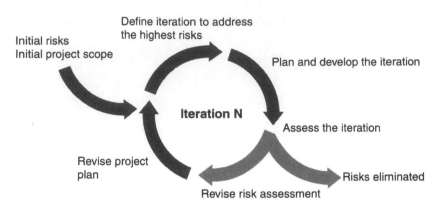

*Figure 12-1    Iteration Planning Process*

### ESU Course Registration Problem Iteration Plan

For the ESU Course Registration problem the iteration plan is as follows:

- Iteration 1
  Maintain professor information
  Select courses to teach
  Maintain curriculum

- Iteration 2
  Maintain student information
  Generate catalog

- Iteration 3
  Register for courses
  Request class roster

---

[3] Booch, Grady. *Object Solutions.* Redwood City, CA: Addison-Wesley, 1995.
[4] *Ibid.*

Iteration 1 addresses the database risk—the courses must be stored in a database that is accessible to all. The *Maintain Professor Info* and *Select Courses to Teach* scenarios are in this iteration since they must be completed before the catalog can be generated. Iteration 2 adds the functionality needed to register a student (the student information must be in the database and the catalog must be available for the students). Iteration 3 completes the system.

## DESIGNING THE USER INTERFACE

EARLIER IN THE project life cycle, placeholder classes were created for the boundary classes for the system. Now, these classes must be finalized—number of windows, window layout, and handling events from users. Sequence diagrams are good sources for user interface requirements. Something in the user interface must provide the capability to receive all "messages" coming from an actor. Something in the user interface must provide the capability to send all "messages" going to an actor.

### *Select Courses to Teach* User Interface Design

The scenarios dealing with the *Select Courses to Teach* use case were examined and the following requirements were found:

- The professor must enter a password to enter the system. A window prompting the professor for a password was created.

- If the password is valid, the ProfessorCourseOptions window is displayed. The ProfessorCourseOptions window contains a field for the semester and for the following buttons: ADD COURSE, DELETE COURSE, REVIEW SCHEDULE, PRINT SCHEDULE.

- Windows for the addition, deletion, and review options were created.

This book concentrates on the design of the ADD COURSE option for the scenario. It is important to note that the design of the system cannot be based on only one scenario—the design matures as more scenarios are developed. I have chosen to use one scenario to illustrate the Rational Unified process and the UML notation that may be used to communicate the design decisions.

The ADD COURSE option deals with adding a professor to a course offering as the teacher. This scenario needs a window to allow the professor to input the needed information—I called it the Addition window. The Addition window contains the following selections:

- Course name field
- Course number field
- Course offerings scroll box
- OK button
- Cancel button
- Quit button

Once the professor enters the course name and number the system will retrieve and display the course offerings. Additionally, the professor will be able to select an offering. When the OK button is pushed, a message is sent to the course object.

The actual implementation of the GUI depends upon the class library chosen and is beyond the scope of this book. This section was included so you would understand the implications of object-oriented GUI design. Most GUI design is accomplished via a GUI builder. In this case, once the GUI classes are created, the reverse engineering capabilities of Rational Rose may be used to add the classes to the model.

## ADDING DESIGN CLASSES

CLASSES ARE TYPICALLY added to the model to facilitate the "how" of a system. For example, the course registration system states that a professor must enter a password that must be validated. A class that knows how to validate passwords is added to the system so this requirement may be implemented. As classes are added to the system, they are displayed on diagrams as needed.

An updated class diagram for the ESU Course Registration problem is shown in Figure 12-2. (Note: At this point in the life cycle, I tend to show stereotypes as a label because I am typically adding a lot of detail to the model. This is just my preference, you do not have to do this. To set stereotype display as a label as the default, select the Tools:Options menu choice, Diagram tab, and label radio button in the Stereotype display field.)

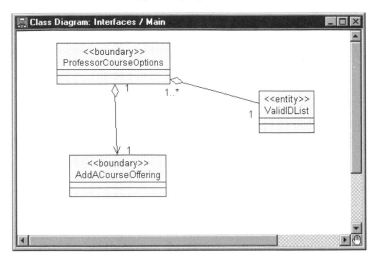

*Figure 12-2   Design Level Class*

## THE EMERGENCE OF PATTERNS

DESIGN PATTERNS PROVIDE solutions to common software design problems. Thus, design patterns may play a part in designing the "how" of a system. In the words of Grady Booch, "patterns are, well, *very cool.*"[5] Patterns provide the capability to reuse successful designs and architectures, which leads to more maintainable systems and increased productivity. As with any classes developed at this point in the life cycle, the classes created to instantiate the design pattern are added to the model and to class diagrams. For example, the Abstract Factory pattern may be used to create the different types of RegistrationUser objects needed. Today, there are many books published with descriptions of design patterns. One of the

[5] Booch, Grady. *Best of Booch, SIGS Reference Library.* New York, NY, 1996, page 167.

most popular books is *Design Patterns: Elements of Reusable Object-Oriented Software* by E. Gamma *et al.*, published by Addison-Wesley in 1995.

## DESIGNING RELATIONSHIPS

THE FOLLOWING DESIGN decisions must be made for relationships: navigation, containment, refinement, and multiplicity implementation.

### Navigation

Associations and aggregations are bidirectional relationships. During design, associations are revisited to determine if bidirectionality is indeed needed. If possible, the relationship is made unidirectional (i.e., navigable in only one direction) since unidirectional relationships are easier to implement and maintain.

SETTING NAVIGATION IN RATIONAL ROSE

1. Right-click at the end of the association or aggregation line to be made non-navigable to make the shortcut menu visible.
2. Click to toggle the Navigation menu choice.

Several unidirectional associations are shown in Figure 12-3.

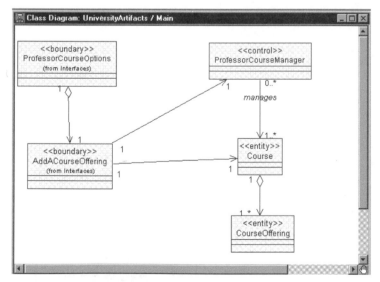

*Figure 12-3    Navigation*

## Containment

Aggregation containment must also be added to the model. Containment may be by value or by reference. Containment by value implies exclusive ownership by the containing class and is shown by a filled diamond. Containment by reference does not mandate exclusive ownership; it is shown by an open diamond.

**SETTING AGGREGATION CONTAINMENT IN RATIONAL ROSE**

1. Double-click on the aggregation line to make the Specification visible.
2. Select the desired Detail tab for the role representing the aggregation whole.
3. Select the desired containment radio button.
4. Click the OK button to close the Specification.

A containment by value relationship (ProfessorCourseOptions contains AddACourseOffering) and a containment by reference relationship (ProfessorCourseOptions to ValidIDList) are shown in Figure 12-4.

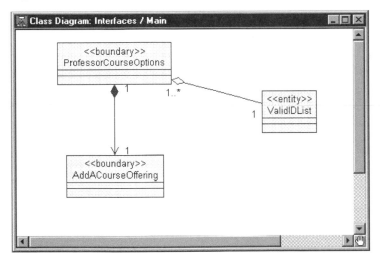

*Figure 12-4   Containment*

## Refinement

An association relationship may be changed into a dependency relationship at this time. A dependency relationship implies that the object requesting the service (client) of another object (supplier) does not have intrinsic knowledge of the location of the supplier object— it must be told where the object is located. Typically, the supplier object is passed as a parameter to one of the methods of the client class or it is declared locally within a method of the client class. A dependency relationship is shown by a dashed arrow pointing from the client to the supplier.

**CREATING DEPENDENCY RELATIONSHIPS IN RATIONAL ROSE**

1. Click to select the Dependency Relationship icon on the toolbar.
2. Click on the class playing the role of the client.
3. Drag the dependency relationship line to the class playing the role of the supplier.

A dependency relationship between CourseOffering and DBCourseOffering is shown in Figure 12-5.

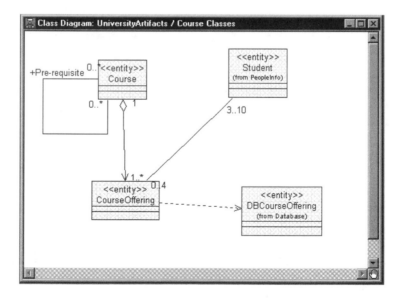

*Figure 12-5   Dependency Relationship*

## Multiplicity Implementation

Multiplicity of one is implemented as an embedded object, a reference, or a pointer. Multiplicity of more than one typically is implemented using a container class (e.g., a set or a list). Again, the list may be an embedded object or a pointer to the container. The decision to update the model to show all the containers that are being used is a tool/project issue. I typically do not show all the containers since they tend to clutter a diagram—instead I use the code generation properties of Rose to set the correct container.

## Relationship Design in the ESU Course Registration Problem

The following relationships must be designed for the *Add a Course to Teach* scenario:

- ProfessorCourseOptions to AddACourseOffering
- ProfessorCourseOptions to ValidIDList
- AddACourseOffering to Course
- Course to CourseOffering
- CourseOffering to Professor
- CourseOffering to DBCourseOffering

## ProfessorCourseOptions to AddACourseOffering

As previously mentioned, the actual design of the GUI class AddACourseOffering is dependent upon the set of GUI controls chosen. The designers have chosen to make the relationship an aggregation by value relationship because the lifetimes of the two windows are dependent. The relationship is navigable from the AddACourseOffering class to the Course class.

## ProfessorCourseOptions to ValidIDList

The ValidIDList is used by many of the windows to validate the input of a user ID. The designers have decided to make this relationship a unidirectional association from ProfessorCourseOptions to ValidIDList.

### AddACourseOffering to Course

This is also a GUI class. The designers have chosen to make the relationship navigable from the AddACourseOffering class to the Course class.

### Course to CourseOffering

This relationship is unidirectional from Course to Course Offering since all messages are in that direction. Additionally, the aggregation is by value because all communication with the Course Offering class is directed through the Course class.

This design implies that a Course and a CourseOffering do not have independent lives. As the requirements for this scenario are stated, this is okay. But let's look at the idea of a Transcript for a student. If a Transcript is just a pointer to the CourseOfferings that a student has taken, this design does not work—the CourseOffering and the Course would have to have independent lives (and the aggregation would be set to "by reference"). Thus, here is a relationship that may mature as more scenarios are designed.

### CourseOffering to Professor

The design based on only this scenario would indicate that the relationship should be a dependency relationship between Course-Offering and Professor since the Professor object is a parameter of the addProfessor operation of the Course Offering class. However, another scenario for this use case is "review schedule." Here, the Professor object must know the related CourseOffering objects, which would imply that the relationship is not a dependency relationship. Finally, the "create catalog" scenario needs to know the assigned Professor for each CourseOffering. This implies that navigation from CourseOffering to Professor is needed. Based on this information, the relationship is not changed—it is a bidirectional association.

### CourseOffering to DBCourseOffering

This relationship may be matured into a dependency relationship because the DBCourseOffering is passed a CourseOffering object as a parameter to the save operation.

The updated class diagrams showing the relationship design are shown in Figures 12-6 and 12-7. This design will probably change as more use cases and scenarios are developed for the system.

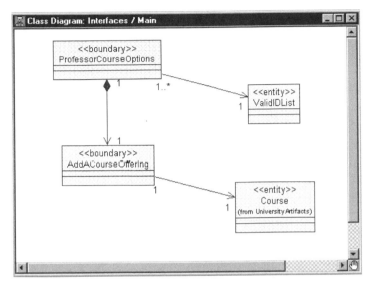

*Figure 12-6   Updated Main Class Diagram for the Interfaces Package*

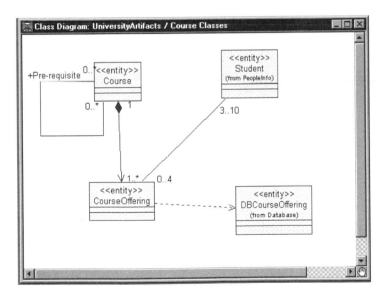

*Figure 12-7   Updated Class Diagram*

## DESIGNING ATTRIBUTES AND OPERATIONS

DURING ANALYSIS, IT was sufficient to specify only attribute and operations names. During design, data types and initial values must be specified for attributes and operations signatures must be supplied. A data type for an attribute may be a language-supplied type such as an integer or it may be a more complex type like a String from a class library. If the attribute must be initialized to a specific value when an object of the class is created, this information is added to the class. In methodology terms, the operation signature includes the parameter list and the return class. Again, parameters and return classes must be assigned a data type. Access control—public, protected, and private—must be set for attributes and operations. Attributes are typically private whereas operations may be private or public. If the class is part of an inheritance hierarchy, attributes and operations may be set to protected to allow access to subclasses.

SETTING ATTRIBUTE DATA TYPES
AND INITIAL VALUES IN RATIONAL ROSE

1.  Right-click to select the class in the browser or on a class diagram and make the shortcut menu visible.
2.  Select the Open Specification menu choice.
3.  Select the Attributes tab.
4.  Click to select the type and place the field in edit mode. Enter the desired type or select a type from the drop-down menu.
5.  Click to select the initial value and place the field in edit mode.  Enter the desired initial value.

SETTING OPERATION SIGNATURES IN RATIONAL ROSE

1.  Right-click to select the class in the browser or on a class diagram and make the shortcut menu visible.
2.  Select the Open Specification menu choice.
3.  Select the Operations tab.
4.  Double-click on an operation to make the Operation Specification visible.
5.  Enter the return class on the General tab.
6.  Select the Detail tab.

7. Right-click in the Arguments field to make the shortcut menu visible.

8. Select the Insert menu choice. This will add an argument. Enter the name, data type, and default value for the argument.

9. Click the OK button to close the Operation Specification.

10. Click the OK button to close the Class Specification.

11. To display the operation signature on a class diagram, either set the display as the default using the Tools:Options menu choice, or the Diagram tab.

12. To display the operation signature on a class by class basis, select the class(es) and choose the Format: Show Operation Signature menu choice.

Note: Attribute and operation detail may also be set on a class diagram by selecting the displayed item and using the following format:

attribute : type = initial value

operation (argname : argtype = default) : return class

Some of the attribute and operation design decisions for the ESU Course Registration problem are shown in Figure 12-8.

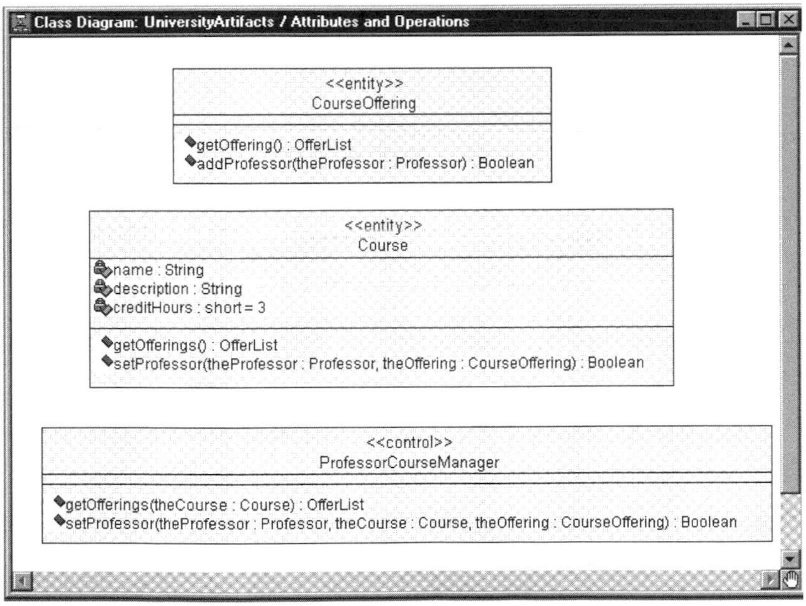

*Figure 12-8  Attribute and Operation Design Details*

## DESIGNING FOR INHERITANCE

DURING ANALYSIS, INHERITANCE hierarchies among key abstractions (i.e., classes) are established. During design, the inheritance hierarchies are refined to

- Increase reuse
- Incorporate design level classes
- Incorporate chosen library classes

Analysis diagrams are reviewed to identify commonality of attributes, operations, and relationships. Superclasses are defined to hold the newly discovered commonality. This reduces the amount of code to be written and tested. It also enforces uniformity; i.e., the same item cannot be handled differently in two different classes if the two classes inherit it from a common superclass.

### Code Generation and Design

The final step of design for an iteration is to add the methods that every good C++ class needs—for example, constructors, destructors, and copy constructors. These method can be added by hand, but this entails a lot of typing. This is why the ability to add these types of methods to a class is found in the Rose code generators.

Rational Rose has very powerful code-generation capabilities. Code is generated based on information obtained from the diagrams, the specifications, and the options specified in the code-generation properties for each type of element. Step-by-step guides to some of the code generation capabilities of Rational Rose may be found in the appendixes.

## CODING, TESTING, AND DOCUMENTING THE ITERATION

ONE OF THE final steps in building an iteration is the implementation of the method bodies in the chosen language before an iteration is complete. Interaction diagrams (Sequence and Collaboration diagrams) are used to help in this process because they tell you who does what to whom and when they do it.

Testing, although it is has not been discussed until this point, is a very important ingredient in the iterative and incremental life cycle. As the analysis and design progresses through the life cycle, testing plans and procedures are created. Again, use cases are an important part of this activity since they document what the system must do. The iteration should be tested to ensure that it truly does what is stated in the use case. Iterations are also integrated with previous iterations—you do not wait until the system is complete to put the iterations together. The iteration is evaluated to ensure that it eliminates its assigned risks. Any risks that were not eliminated (along with any risks that were found along the way) are reassigned to a future iteration.

The decisions made regarding the design of the iteration are captured in the models for the iteration. This information is used to generate the documentation for the iteration. Documentation should be generated on a iterative basis—I have found that systems that wait until the project is complete to document it rarely have good documentation (indeed, they sometimes do not have any documentation!).

## USING REVERSE ENGINEERING TO SET THE STAGE FOR THE NEXT ITERATION

THE MODEL MUST be updated to reflect any changes made to the code (c.g., helping methods added, new classes added) while implementing the current iteration. Rather than updating the model by hand, the reverse engineering capability of Rose can be used to generate a model based on the current implementation, and this information can be merged into the model. Step-by-step guides to reverse engineering with Rational Rose 2000 may be found in the appendixes.

## SUMMARY

THE ITERATION RELEASE plan prescribes schedules for all the increments of the system. The scenarios developed during analysis are the main input to this phase of development. The scenarios are examined and prioritized according to risk, importance to the customer, and the need to develop certain basic scenarios first. As each iteration is completed, risks are reevaluated and the project plan is updated as needed.

Earlier in the project life cycle, placeholder classes were created for the boundary classes for the system. Now, these classes must be finalized—number of windows, window layout, and handling events from users. Classes typically are added to the model to facilitate the "how" of a system. Patterns provide the capability to reuse successful designs and architectures, which leads to more maintainable systems and increased productivity. As with any classes developed at this point in the life cycle, the classes created to instantiate the design pattern are added to the model and to the class diagram. Relationship design decisions include navigation, containment, refinement, and multiplicity implementation. Attribute data types and initial values are specified. Operation signatures are finalized. Analysis level diagrams are examined to determine if any inheritance may be added to the model. Operations in inheritance hierarchies are analyzed to determine if any polymorphism exists. If so, the operation is made either virtual or pure virtual.

The final step of design for an iteration is to add the methods that every good class needs—for example, constructors, destructors, and copy constructors if the chosen language is C++. Rational Rose has very powerful code-generation capabilities. Code is generated based on information obtained from the diagrams, the specifications, and the options specified in the code-generation properties for each type of element.

Finally, the method bodies are implemented in the chosen language. Each iteration should be tested and documented before it is considered completed. The iteration is evaluated and any unmitigated risks are assigned to a future release.

# Code Generation and Reverse Engineering with C++

THIS APPENDIX CONTAINS a step-by-step guide to Classic C++ code generation and reverse engineering. This generator is not turned on by default. To turn it on, select the Add-Ins: Add In Manager menu choice, select the Rose C++ add-in and click the OK button.

### Code Generation Steps

Step 1: Create Needed Property Sets
Step 2: Create Body Components in the Component Diagram
Step 3: Assign the C++ Language to the Components
Step 4: Assign Classes to Components
Step 5: Attach Property Sets to Modeling Elements
Step 6: Select the Components and Generate the Code
Step 7: Evaluate the Code Generation Errors

### Reverse Engineering Steps

Step 1: Create a Project
Step 2: Add a Project Caption
Step 3: Add Referenced Libraries and Base Projects
Step 4: Set the File Type and Analyze the Files
Step 5: Evaluate the Errors
Step 6: Select Export Options and Export to Rose
Step 7: Update Rose Model

## CODE GENERATION

### Step 1: Create Needed Property Sets

There are code-generation properties associated with the project, the class, roles, attributes, and operations. The properties applying to the project as a whole involve file name, default container names, and placement of the generated code. Class properties involve the generation of constructors, destructors, copy constructors, equality operators, and get/set methods. The property set for roles deals with the construction of get/set methods, visibility of the methods, and the container class to be used. Operation properties deal with the operation kind (common, virtual, abstract, static, or friend) and allow the operation to be made constant. These property sets may be edited, and new sets may be created to specify the C++ features needed for the project. Two files are generated for each class—a header (.h) file and a specification (.cpp) file.

For a typical project, a few people are responsible for the creation of code generation property sets that are used by the entire development team. This enables each developer to generate the needed code for the components. Some typical property sets are Virtual destructor, Virtual operation, Abstract operation, Static operation, No get member function, and Forward reference.

**CREATING PROPERTY SETS IN RATIONAL ROSE**
1.  Select the Tools:Options menu choice.
2.  Select the C++ tab.
3.  Click the arrow in the Type field to make the drop-down menu visible.
4.  Select the desired type of property set.
5.  Click the Clone button to make the Clone Property Set window visible.
6.  Enter the name of the new property set.
7.  Click the OK button to close the Clone Property Set window.
8.  Click to select the property to change.
9.  Click the value.
10.  Enter the new value or select the new value from the drop-down menu if one is provided.
11.  Repeat steps 8 through 10 for each property to be changed.
12.  Click the Apply button to apply the changes.
13.  Repeat the preceding steps for each new property set.
14.  Click the OK button to close the Options window.

The property set Virtual Destructor is shown in Figure A-1.

**Step 2: Create Body Components in the Component Diagram**
Rational Rose generates code based on the components and their stereotypes present in the diagram. For components without a stereotype, Rose will generate a .h file containing definition and declaration information for the class. For components with a stereotype of

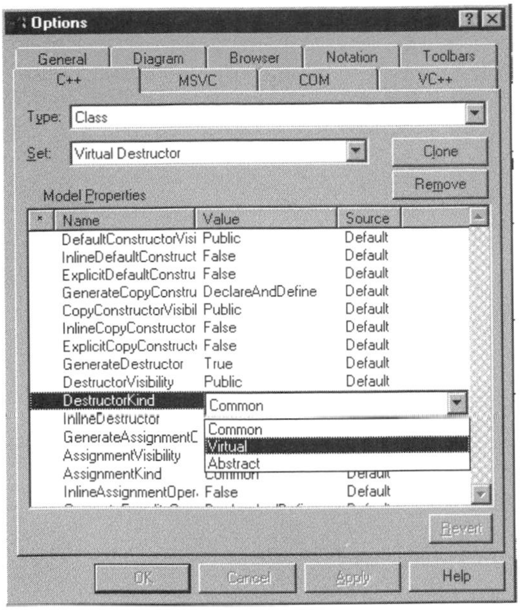

*Figure A-1   Virtual Destructor Property Set*

Package Specification, Rose will generate a .h file containing the definition information for the class. If there is a corresponding component with a stereotype of Package Body, Rose will generate a .cpp file containing declaration information for the class.

**ASSIGNING STEREOTYPES TO COMPONENTS IN RATIONAL ROSE**

1. Double-click on a component diagram to open the diagram.
2. Click right on the component to make the shortcut menu visible.
3. Select the Open Specification menu command.
4. Enter the desired stereotype in the stereotype field or click the arrow in the Stereotype field to make the drop-down menu visible and select the desired stereotype.
5. Click the OK button to close the Specification.

The Component Specification is shown in Figure A-2.

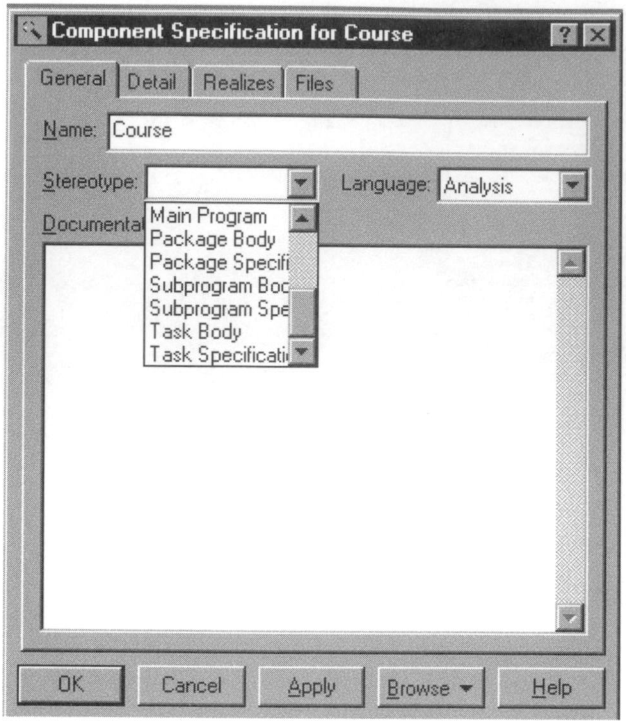

**Component Specification for Course**   ? ✕

| General | Detail | Realizes | Files |

Name: Course

Stereotype: [           ▼]     Language: [Analysis ▼]

Documenta| Main Program        ▲
          | Package Body
          | Package Specifi
          | Subprogram Boc
          | Subprogram Spe
          | Task Body
          | Task Specificati ▼

[ OK ]   [ Cancel ]   [ Apply ]   [ Browse ▼ ]   [ Help ]

*Figure A-2   Component Specification*

**CREATING COMPONENT HEADERS AND BODIES
IN RATIONAL ROSE**

1. Double-click on a component diagram to open the diagram.
2. Click right on the component to make the shortcut menu visible.
3. Select the Open Specification menu command.
4. To create a stereotype for a header file, select the Package Specification stereotype.
5. To create a stereotype for a component body, select the Package Body stereotype.
6. Click the OK button to close the Specification.

A component diagram with components for C + + .h and .cpp files is shown in Figure A-3.

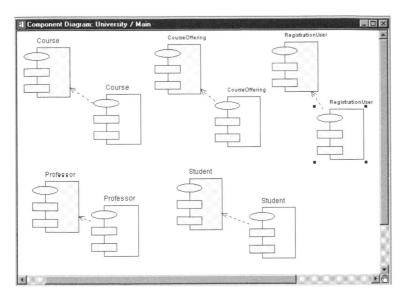

*Figure A-3   Updated Component Diagram*

### Step 3: Assign the C + + Language to the Components

Once the components for the header and body are created, they must be assigned the C + + language. If the default language for a model is set to C + + (Tools:Options menu, notation tab), Rational Rose automatically will assign the C + + to components in the model.

**ASSIGNING A LANGUAGE TO A COMPONENT**
**IN RATIONAL ROSE**

1. Right-click to select the component in the Browser or on a diagram and make the shortcut menu visible.
2. Select the Open Specification menu command.
3. Click the arrow in the Language field to make the drop-down menu visible.
4. Select C + +.
5. Click the OK button to close the Specification.

The Component Specification for the Course class is shown in Figure A-4.

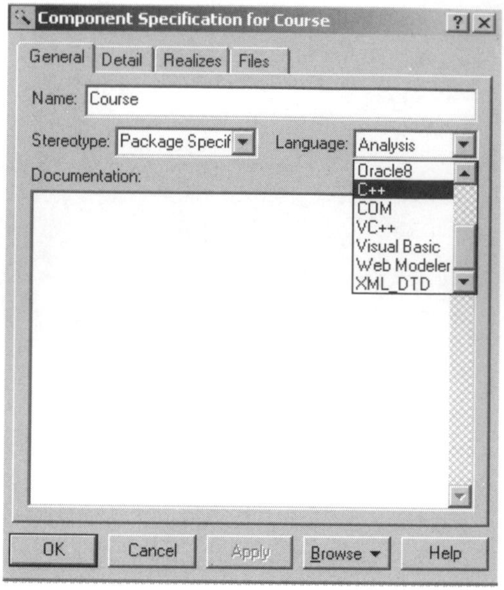

**Component Specification for Course**                ? X

General | Detail | Realizes | Files |

Name: Course

Stereotype: Package Specif ▼   Language: Analysis ▼

Documentation:
                               Oracle8
                               C++
                               COM
                               VC++
                               Visual Basic
                               Web Modeler
                               XML_DTD ▼

OK     Cancel     Apply     Browse ▼     Help

*Figure A-4    Assigning a Language to a Component*

### Step 4: Assign Classes to Components

Once components have been created, classes are assigned to the components representing the header file.

**ASSIGNING CLASSES TO COMPONENTS IN
RATIONAL ROSE**

1. Double-click on the component diagram containing the components representing the .h and .cpp files to open the diagram.
2. Click to select the class in the Browser and drag it onto the component representing the .h file.

### Step 5: Attach Property Sets to Modeling Elements

Each modeling element (e.g., class, attribute, or role) is examined to determine its code needs. If a property set other than the default set is needed, it is attached to the modeling element.

**ATTACHING A PROPERTY SET TO A SELECTED**
**ELEMENT IN RATIONAL ROSE**

1. Right-click to select the element in the Browser or on a diagram and make the shortcut menu visible.
2. Select the Open Specification menu choice.
3. Select the C++ tab.
4. Click the arrow in the Set field to make the drop-down menu visible.
5. Select the desired property set.
6. Click the OK button to close the Specification.

The property set VirtualDestructor has been attached to the RegistrationUser class as shown in Figure A-5.

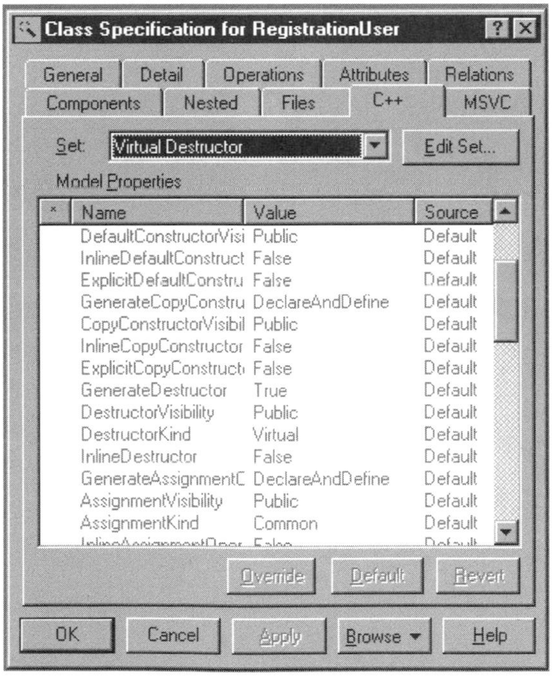

*Figure A-5   Property Set Attachment*

Since there are not property sets for every combination of elements, any property may also be overridden for a particular element. This is true even if the property is part of the default property set for the element.

**OVERRIDING A PROPERTY IN RATIONAL ROSE**

1.  Right-click to select the element in the Browser or on a diagram and make the shortcut menu visible.
2.  Select the Open Specification menu choice.
3.  Select the C++ tab.
4.  Click the arrow in the Set field to make the drop-down menu visible.
5.  Select the desired property set.
6.  Click to select the value to be changed.
7.  Enter the new value or select the new value from the drop-down menu if one is provided.
8.  Repeat steps 6 and 7 for each property to be changed.
9.  Click the OK button to close the specification button.

## Step 6: Select the Components and Generate the Code

Code may be generated for an entire package, a component, or a set of components. The name of the component is used to generate the name of the file containing the code. The code is placed in a directory structure that corresponds to the package names in the component view.

**GENERATING CODE IN RATIONAL ROSE**

1.  Click to select the package, component, or set of components.
2.  Select the Tools:C++:Code Generation menu choice.
3.  Rose will display the status in the Code Generation Status window.

The Code Generation Status window is shown in Figure A-6.

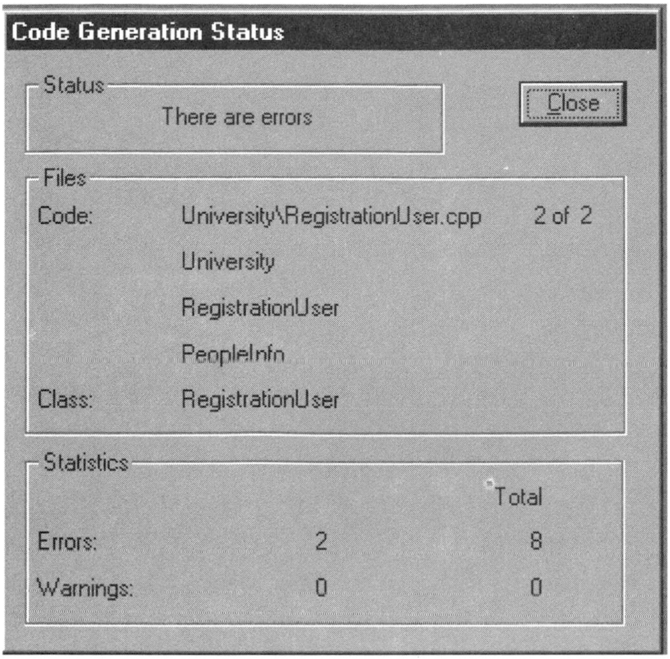

*Figure A-6    Code Generation Status*

## Step 7: Evaluate the Code Generation Errors

Rose writes all warnings and errors to the Log window. If a part
of the design for the class is not complete, Rose will write a warning message to the log and use a default value. This is especially
important if an iterative approach to development is being followed
since an entire class may not be implemented in one iteration.

The common warnings and errors output from the code
generator are

- ■ Error: Missing attribute data type. Void is assumed.

- ■ Warning: Unspecified multiplicity/cardinality indicators.
  One is assumed.

- ■ Warning: Missing operation return type. Void is assumed.

The Log window is shown in Figure A-7.

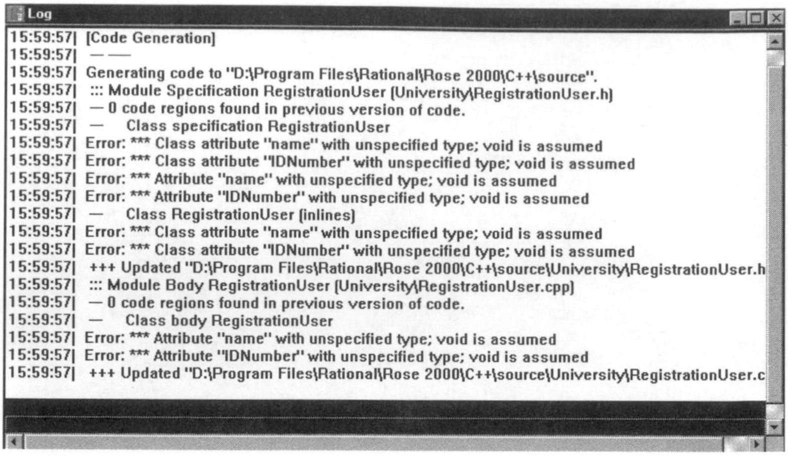

```
Log                                                                          _ □ ×
15:59:57|  [Code Generation]
15:59:57|  — —
15:59:57|  Generating code to "D:\Program Files\Rational\Rose 2000\C++\source".
15:59:57|  ::: Module Specification RegistrationUser [University\RegistrationUser.h]
15:59:57|  — 0 code regions found in previous version of code.
15:59:57|  —    Class specification RegistrationUser
15:59:57|  Error: *** Class attribute "name" with unspecified type; void is assumed
15:59:57|  Error: *** Class attribute "IDNumber" with unspecified type; void is assumed
15:59:57|  Error: *** Attribute "name" with unspecified type; void is assumed
15:59:57|  Error: *** Attribute "IDNumber" with unspecified type; void is assumed
15:59:57|  —    Class RegistrationUser [inlines]
15:59:57|  Error: *** Class attribute "name" with unspecified type; void is assumed
15:59:57|  Error: *** Class attribute "IDNumber" with unspecified type; void is assumed
15:59:57|  +++ Updated "D:\Program Files\Rational\Rose 2000\C++\source\University\RegistrationUser.h
15:59:57|  ::: Module Body RegistrationUser [University\RegistrationUser.cpp]
15:59:57|  — 0 code regions found in previous version of code.
15:59:57|  —    Class body RegistrationUser
15:59:57|  Error: *** Attribute "name" with unspecified type; void is assumed
15:59:57|  Error: *** Attribute "IDNumber" with unspecified type; void is assumed
15:59:57|  +++ Updated "D:\Program Files\Rational\Rose 2000\C++\source\University\RegistrationUser.c
```

*Figure A-7   Rational Rose Log Window*

## REVERSE ENGINEERING USING THE C++ ANALYZER

### Step 1: Create a Project

A C++ Analyzer project contains the information needed to extract a Rose design from source-code files. An analyzer project contains the following information:

- Caption: Informational description of the project.

- Directories: List of directories used by the Analyzer. The directories that contain the source code files as well as the directories containing any code used by the source code to be analyzed must be included in the directory list.

- Extensions: List of file extensions recognized by the analyzer.

- Files: List of files to be analyzed.

- Defined Symbols and Undefined Symbols: List of preprocessor symbols and their expansions.

- Categories: List of packages to which classes and packages may be assigned.

- Subsystems: List of packages to which components and packages may be assigned.

- Bases: List of base projects containing information needed to resolve source code references.

- Type 2 Context: Preprocessor directives needed by context-sensitive source code files.

- Export Options: List of information that is to be exported either to create or update a Rose model.

Once a project is created, it is saved with a .pjt extension.

**CREATING A PROJECT IN THE C++ ANALYZER**

1. Select the Tools:C++:Reverse Engineering menu choice to start the C++ Analyzer.
2. Select the File:New menu choice.

The C++ Analyzer Project window is shown in Figure A-8.

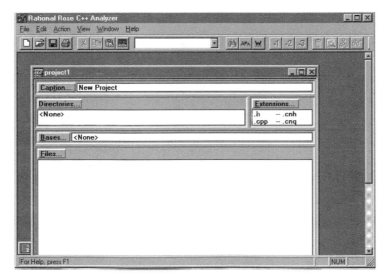

*Figure A-8   C++ Analyzer Project Window*

## Step 2: Add Project Caption

Just as code is documented for future use, analyzer projects are also documented. Each project should contain a caption. This is typically descriptive information about the project such as its title and purpose. This information may be used by other teams to determine if the project has reuse potential either as a standalone project or as a base project.

ADDING A CAPTION IN THE C++ ANALYZER

1.  Click the Caption button to make the Caption window visible.
2.  Enter the information in the Caption window.
3.  Click the OK button to close the Caption window.

The Caption window is shown in Figure A-9.

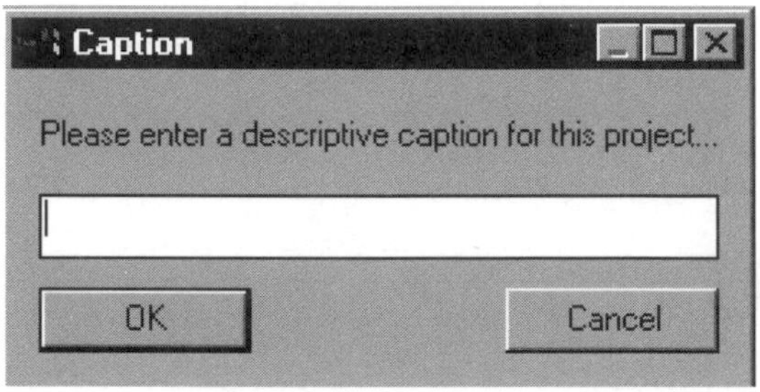

*Figure A-9   Caption Window*

## Step 3: Add Referenced Libraries and Base Projects

The directory list contains a list of directories used by the C++ Analyzer. The directory containing a file to be analyzed must be in the directory list. In addition, the directory for any included file must also be in the directory list.

**CREATING THE DIRECTORY LIST IN THE C++ ANALYZER**

1. Click the Directories button to make the Project Directory List window visible.
2. Click to select a directory in the Directory Structure file. This will set the directory to the current directory.
3. Click the Add Current button to add the current directory to the directory list.
4. Click the Add Subdirs button to add the current directory and its immediate subdirectories to the directory list.
5. Click the Add Hierarchy button to add the current directory and all its nested subdirectories to the directory list.

The Project Directory List window is shown in Figure A-10.

*Figure A-10   Project Directory List Window*

An analyzer project may use information from another project, called a base project. Typically, base projects contain information about header files for compiler-specific libraries or class libraries on which the program is built. Rather than reanalyze this information in every project that uses these files, a base project is created. The base project may then be used by any other project that needs information about the files in the base project. Base projects are identified in the base project list.

If the Analyzer cannot find a file in the project directory list, it will look for the file in a base project, which are searched in the order in which they appear in the base project list.

**ADDING BASE PROJECTS IN THE C++ ANALYZER**

1. Click the Bases button to make the Base Projects window visible.
2. Click to navigate through the directory structure until the desired project is visible in the File Name box.
3. Click to select the project.
4. Click the Add button to add the base project.

The Base Projects window is shown in Figure A-11.

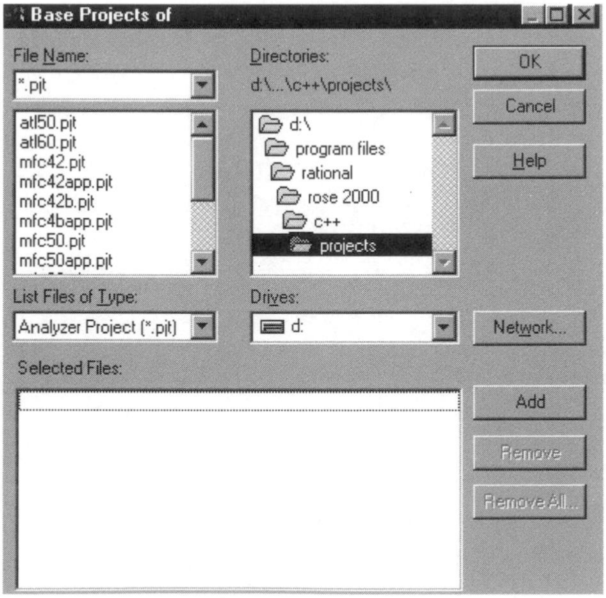

![Base Projects window screenshot]

*Figure A-11   Base Projects Window*

## Step 4: Set the File Type and Analyze the Files

The analyzer categorizes files into three different file types—Type 1, Type 2, and Type 3. When a file is added to the file list it is made a Type 1 file. This type of file is syntactically complete and context independent. That is, the file is a list of complete C++ declarations at file scope and either contains all information that it needs or obtains the information from its #include directives. A Type 2 file is syntactically complete but context-dependent; that is, the file is a list of complete C++ declarations at file scope but the file contains symbols whose definitions are provided by the context in which it is included. A Type 3 file is syntactically incomplete. Type 3 files are always processed as they are encountered.

TO CHANGE THE ANALYSIS TYPE IN THE C++ ANALYZER

1. Click to select the file in the files list.
2. Click to select the appropriate type from the Action:Set Type menu.

The C++ Analyzer may process a single file or a group of files. The Analyzer creates and stores analysis information in a data file for each file it processes. This data may be used the next time the file is analyzed. The status of each file is updated in the files list as the file is processed. The status may be

- Unknown: The file has not been analyzed.

- Stale Data: There is potentially out-of-date data for the file.

- Analyzed: Successful analysis. This status is applied to Type 1 and Type 2 source code files only.

- CodeCycled: Successful analysis, and the file contains annotations that protect existing information in the code from being overwritten. This status is applied to Type 1 and Type 2 source code files only.

- Excluded: This is a Type 3 file, which is analyzed each time it is encountered in another file.

- Has Errors: Found errors in the source code file while analyzing it.

- No Source: Cannot find the file in the file system.

- Unanalyzed: Cannot find a data file for this file.

**ANALYZING FILES IN THE C++ ANALYZER**

1. Set the Analysis Type for each file to be analyzed.
2. Click to select the files in the Files list.
3. Select the Action:Analyze menu choice to analyze the file, or select the Action:CodeCycle menu choice to analyze the file and ensure that the annotations needed for Rose are present.

The analyzer window along with an analysis status is shown in Figure A-12.

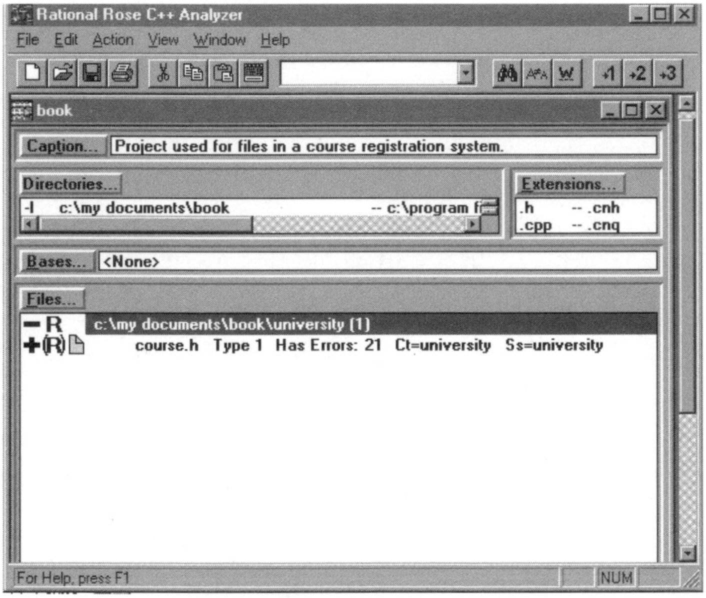

*Figure A-12   Analyzer Status*

### Step 5: Evaluate the Errors

The Analyzer writes all errors to the Log window. Errors can also be viewed in the files list by double-clicking on the file. Each error should be evaluated as to its severity. Some common errors are

- Unresolved references: The Analyzer cannot find referenced source files. To resolve this type of error, the directory containing the referenced source file must be added to the directory list.

- Missing language extensions: Language extensions not recognized by the Analyzer. To resolve this type of error, the language extension must be defined as a symbol.

- Context-sensitive source files: Code from another directory is referenced but not included in the file. To resolve this type of error, change the file to either a Type 2 or Type 3 file.

The analyzer window, along with the errors encountered during analysis, is shown in Figure A-13.

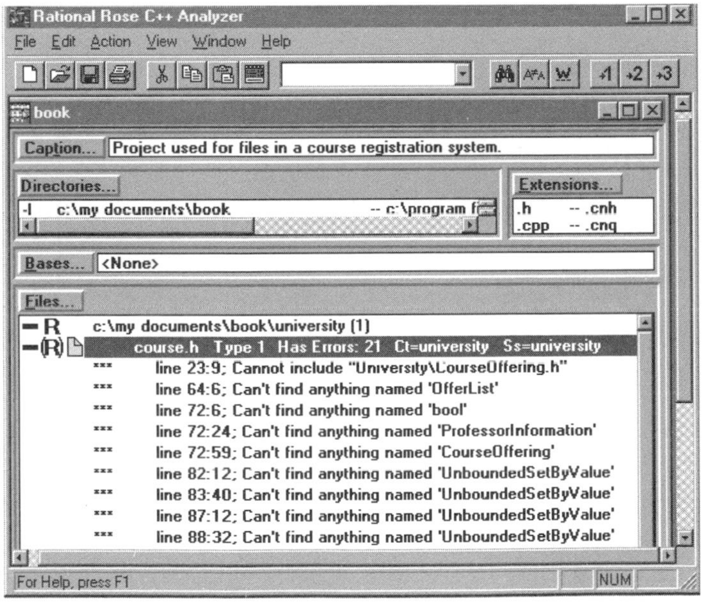

*Figure A-13   Analyzer Errors*

### Step 6: Select Export Options and Export to Rose

The export options specify what elements should be modeled and drawn in the exported file. For example, a class can be modeled and drawn, comments can be added, associations can be modeled and drawn, and dependency relationships can be modeled. If an element is modeled and drawn, it will be visible in the created or updated Rose model. If an element is modeled, it can be drawn within Rose once a Rose model is created or updated. If it is not modeled, then it can never be drawn in Rose.

The C++ Analyzer has multiple export options sets already set up for your use. They are

- RoundTrip: Export options useful in a round-trip engineering exercise. A file with the extension .red is created.

- First Look: High-level look at the model. A .mdl file is created.

- DetailedAnalysis: Detailed look at the model. A .mdl file is created.

You have the option of using one of the preexisting export option sets, modifying one of the preexisting export option sets, or creating your own export option set.

**EXPORTING TO ROSE IN THE C++ ANALYZER**

1. Click to select the files to be exported.
2. Select the Action:Export to Rose menu choice.
3. Click the arrow on the Option Set field to make the drop-down menu visible.
4. Click to select the desired export option set.
5. Click the OK button or the Overwrite button to export to Rose.

The Export to Rose window is shown in Figure A-14.

**Export To Rose**

File: `c:\program files\rational\rational rose c++ 4.0\cour`  Browse...

Title: `Project used for files in a course registration system.`

Option Set: `RoundTrip`   Mk Dflt   Edit...

Summary of Options

```
Option Set              : RoundTrip
Design Title            : %c
Model File              : $DESIGN/%f.red
Notation                : Booch
Export Scope            : Selected Only
Search Effort           : Project and Bases
--- Category Options...
Categories              : from Annotations; Mode
Category Units          : All in Design File;
Category File Extension  . cat
--- Subsystem Options...
```

OK    Cancel              Overwrite    Help

*Figure A-14   Export to Rose*

## Step 7: Update Rose Model

Once the .red file is created by the Analyzer, it is used to update the
Rose model. This will replace elements of the Rose model with elements extracted from the source code. In addition, any elements in
the code that are not in the model are added to the model.

**UPDATING A ROSE MODEL**

1. Open the Rose model to be updated.
2. Select the File:Update menu choice.
3. Navigate through the directory structure to locate
   the .red file.
4. Click to select the .red file.
5. Click the OK button to close the Update Model From
   window.

# Code Generation and Reverse Engineering with Visual C++ and Visual Basic

THIS APPENDIX CONTAINS a step-by-step guide to Visual C+ + and Visual Basic code generation and reverse engineering.

### Code Generation Steps

Step 1: Assign the Visual C+ + or Visual Basic Language to the components

Step 2: Assign classes to components

Step 3: Use the Model Assistant Tool to set code generation properties

Step 4: Select the components and use the Code Update Tool to generate the code

Step 5: Evaluate the code generation errors

### Reverse Engineering Steps

Step 1: Use the Model Update Tool to reverse engineer the Visual C+ + or Visual Basic code

Step 2: Evaluate the errors

## CODE GENERATION

### Step 1: Assign the Visual C+ + or Visual Basic Language to the Components

Components must be assigned a language. The language of a component is set for all classes assigned to the component.

ASSIGNING A LANGUAGE TO A COMPONENT IN RATIONAL ROSE

1. Right-click to select the component in the Browser or on a diagram and make the shortcut menu visible.

2. Select the Open Specification menu command.

3. Click the arrow in the Language field to make the drop-down menu visible.

4. Select the desired language.

5. Click the OK button to close the Specification.

The Component Specification for the ProfessorCourseOptions component is shown in Figure B-1.

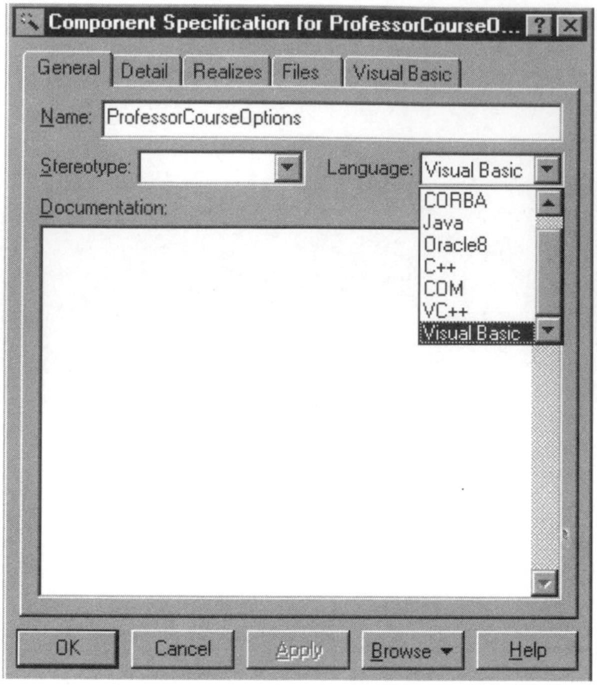

**Component Specification for ProfessorCourseO...** ? ✕

| General | Detail | Realizes | Files | Visual Basic |

Name: ProfessorCourseOptions

Stereotype: [            ▼]    Language: [Visual Basic ▼]

Documentation:
```
CORBA
Java
Oracle8
C++
COM
VC++
Visual Basic
```

[ OK ]  [ Cancel ]  [ Apply ]  [ Browse ▼ ]  [ Help ]

*Figure B-1   Component Specification*

## Step 2: Assign Classes to Components

Once components have been created, classes are assigned to the components.  The components represent either a Visual C++ or a Visual Basic project.

**ASSIGNING CLASSES TO COMPONENTS IN RATIONAL ROSE**
1. Right-click on the component in the Browser or on a Component Diagram to make the shortcut menu visible.
2. Select the Open Specification menu choice.
3. Select the Realizes tab.
4. Right-click on the class to be assigned to the component to make the shortcut menu visible.
5. Select the Assign menu choice.
6. Repeat steps 4 and 5 for each class to be assigned to the component.

The component specification for the ProfessorCourseOptions component is shown in Figure B-2.

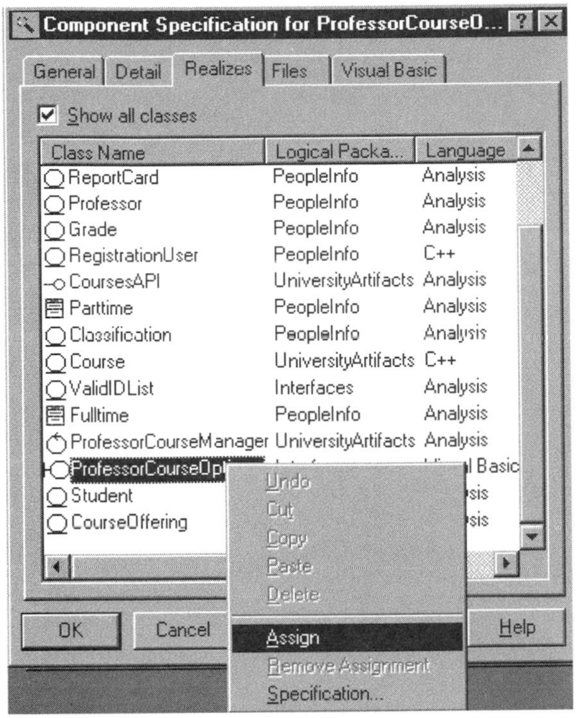

*Figure B-2    Realizes Tab of a Component Specification*

## Step 3: Use the Model Assistant Tool to Set Code Generation Properties

The Model Assistant Tool maps modeling elements in Rational Rose to Visual C++ or Visual Basic constructs. In Visual Basic, the Model Assistant Tool may be used to create and specify constants, declare statements, event statements, enum and type declarations, properties, methods, and method parameters. It also allows you to create Get, Let, and Set procedures for class properties and association roles, and to define and create a user-defined collection class for the class. In Visual C++, the Model Assistant Tool may be used to create and specify class operations like constructors and destructors as well as accessor operations for the attributes and relationships.

The Preview field displays the code to be generated for a selected member.  This allows you to see how your code generation settings will be applied to the member.

The Model Assistant is available for when

- The default language for a model is set to Visual Basic or Visual C++

- The class is assigned to a Visual Basic or Visual C++ component

Detailed information about the Model Assistant Tool may be found in the Rational Rose Help files.

**TO START THE MODEL ASSISTANT TOOL**

1. Right-click to select the class in the Browser or on a class diagram and make the shortcut menu visible.
2. Select the Model Assistant menu choice.

The Model Assistant Tool for a class assigned the Visual Basic language is shown in Figure B-3.  The Model Assistant Tool for a class assigned the Visual C++ language is shown in Figure B-4.

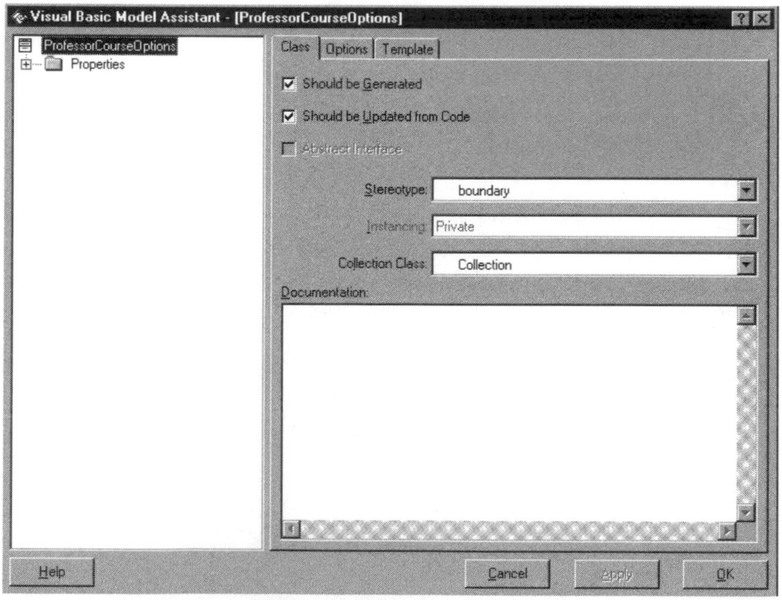

*Figure B-3    Visual Basic Model Assistant*

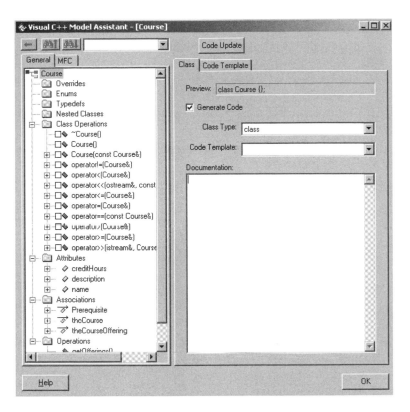

*Figure B-4    Visual C + + Model Assistant*

## Step 4: Select the Components and Use the Code Update Tool to Generate the Code

The Code Update Tool is used to generate the Visual C + +
or Visual Basic code. Code may be generated for all components
in a package, a single component, or a set of components.

TO START THE CODE UPDATE TOOL

1.  Right-click on the component in the Browser or on
    a component diagram to make the shortcut menu
    visible.
2.  Select the Update Code menu choice.

The Code Update tool is shown in Figure B-5.

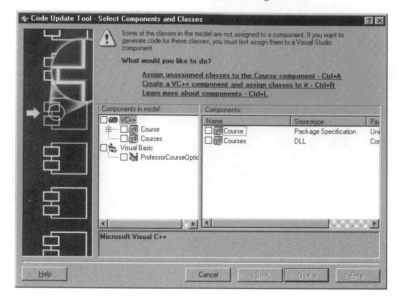

*Figure B-5    Code Update Tool*

Detailed information about the Code Update tool may be found in the Rose Help files.

### Step 5: Evaluate the Code Generation Errors

When the code generation process is complete, the Summary window is displayed in the Code Update tool. The Summary tab contains information about the generated code and all code generation errors are written to the Log, which can be viewed by selecting the Log tab of the Summary window.

The Summary window is shown in Figure B-6.

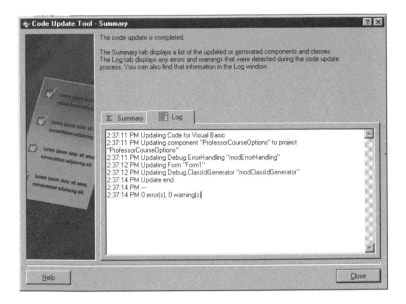

*Figure B-6   Summary Window*

## REVERSE ENGINEERING

### Step 1: Use the Model Update Tool to Reverse Engineer the Visual C+ + or Visual Basic Code

Once you complete your code in Visual C+ + or Visual Basic you need to update the model to reflect any changes. This can be accomplished by using the Model Update tool. You can also use this tool to create an initial model for existing code.

TO UPDATE (CREATE) A MODEL FROM CODE USING THE
MODEL UPDATE TOOL

    1.  Select the Tools:Visual C+ +:Update Model from
        Code or the Tools:Visual Basic:Update Model from
        Code menu command.

    2.  Follow the steps of the wizard.

The Model Update Tool is shown in Figure B-7.

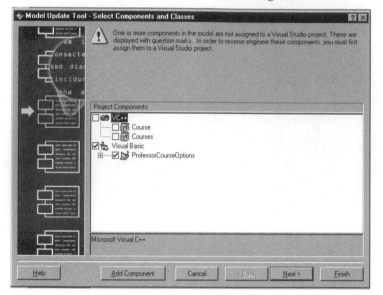

*Figure B-7    Model Update Tool*

### Step 2:  Evaluate the Errors

When the reverse engineering process is complete, the Summary window is displayed in the Model Update tool.   The Summary tab contains information about the generated code and all code generation errors are written to the Log, which can be viewed by selecting the Log tab of the Summary window.

The Summary window is shown in Figure B-8.

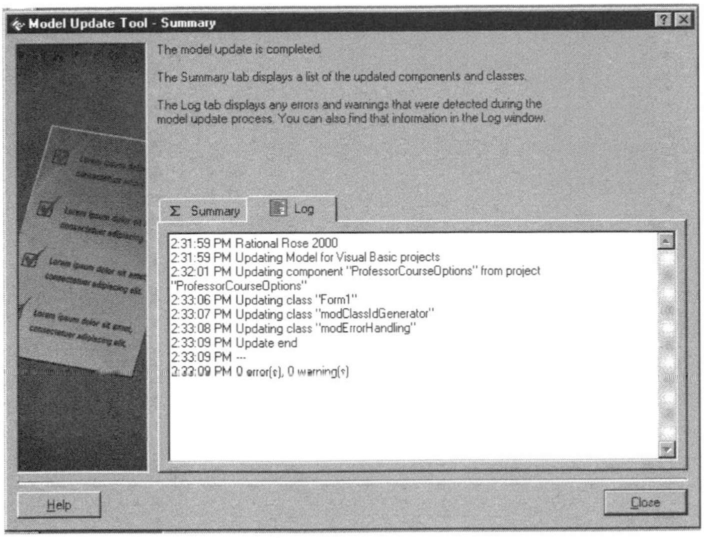

*Figure B-8   Summary Window*

Appendix C

# A Visual Basic Example

THIS APPENDIX SHOWS all the steps necessary to build a Visual Basic DLL and then use the DLL in an application (this means that you must have Rational Rose Enterprise or Rational Rose Professional Visual Basic Edition). If Visual Basic is not an available language, select the Add-Ins: Add-In Manager menu choice, select the Visual Basic add-in, and click the OK button to close the Add-In Manager window. Since there is usually more than one way to do something in Rational Rose, I will vary how I create an element in this example.

## MAKE AN ACTIVEX DLL

### SET THE DEFAULT LANGUAGE TO VISUAL BASIC AND THE STEREOTYPE DISPLAY TO LABEL

1. Select the Tools:Options menu command.
2. Select the Notation tab.
3. Click the arrow in the Default Language field to make the drop-down menu visible.
4. Select Visual Basic.
5. Select the Diagram tab.
6. Select the Label radio button in the Stereotype Display field.
7. Click the OK button to close the Options window.

### SET VISUAL BASIC CODE GENERATION OPTIONS

1. Select the Tools:Visual Basic:Properties menu command.
2. Deselect the Generate debug code and the Generate error-handling code checkboxes.
3. Click the OK button to close the Visual Basic Properties window.

### CREATE THE PAYCLERK CLASS

1. Click the + next to the Logical View package in the Browser to expand the view.
2. Double-click on the diagram called Main to open the diagram.
3. Select the Class icon on the toolbar.
4. Click on the Main class diagram to create the class.
5. While the class is still selected, enter its name . . . Payclerk.

**GIVE THE PAYCLERK DOCUMENTATION AND AN OPERATION**

1. Double-click on the class on either the Main class diagram or in the Browser to open the Class Specification.
2. Enter the documentation for the Payclerk in the Documentation field . . . a Payclerk calculates weekly pay.
3. Select the Operations tab.
4. Right-click to make the shortcut menu visible.
5. Select the Insert menu choice. This will insert an operation called opname.
6. While the operation is still selected, enter its name . . . calcPay.
7. Click the OK button to close the Class Specification.

**SET THE ARGUMENTS AND RETURN TYPE FOR THE CALCPAY OPERATION**

1. Click the + next to the Logical View package in the Browser to expand the package.
2. Click the + next to the Payclerk class in the Browser to expand the class.
3. Double-click on the calcPay operation to make the Operation Specification visible.
4. Click the arrow in the Return class field to make the drop-down menu visible.
5. Select Currency.
6. Select the Detail tab.
7. Right-click in the Arguments field to make the shortcut menu visible.
8. Select the Insert menu choice. This will insert an argument called argname.
9. While the new argument is still selected, enter its name . . . rate.
10. Click the Type field to make the drop-down menu visible.
11. Select Integer.
12. Click the OK button to close the Operation Specification.

### CREATE THE IPAYROLL INTERFACE CLASS

1. Right-click on the Logical View package in the Browser to make the shortcut menu visible.
2. Select the New: Interface menu choice. This will insert a new class with a Stereotype of Interface in the Browser.
3. While the new interface class is still selected, enter its name . . . IPayroll.

### ADD THE INTERFACE CLASS TO THE MAIN CLASS DIAGRAM

1. Open the Main class diagram by double-clicking on the diagram called Main in the Logical View package of the Browser.
2. Click to select the IPayroll class in the Browser.
3. Drag the class onto the Main class diagram.

### ADD AN OPERATION TO THE IPAYROLL CLASS

1. Right-click on the IPayroll class on the Main class diagram to make the shortcut menu visible.
2. Select the New:Operation menu choice. This will add a new operation called opname to the class.
3. While the new operation is still selected, enter its name and return type . . . calcPay(rate:Integer):Currency (make sure you use this format).

### CREATE THE PAYROLL CLASS

1. Right-click on the Logical View package in the Browser to make the shortcut menu visible.
2. Select the New: Class menu choice. This will insert a new class in the Browser.
3. While the new class is still selected, enter its name . . . Payroll.

**ADD THE PAYROLL CLASS TO THE MAIN CLASS DIAGRAM**

1. Open the Main class diagram by double-clicking on the diagram called Main in the Logical View package of the Browser.
2. Click to select the Payroll class in the Browser.
3. Drag the class onto the Main class diagram.

**CREATE A REALIZE RELATIONSHIP BETWEEN THE IPAYROLL CLASS AND THE PAYROLL CLASS**

1. Click to select the Realize icon on the toolbar.
2. Click on the Payroll class on the Main class diagram and drag the association to the IPayroll class.

**CREATE A RELATIONSHIP BETWEEN THE PAYROLL CLASS AND THE PAYCLERK CLASS**

1. Click to select the Unidirectional Association icon on the toolbar.
2. Click on the Payroll class on the Main class diagram and drag the association to the Payclerk class.

**CREATE A ROLL NAME**

1. Right-click on the association near the Payclerk class to make the shortcut menu visible.
2. Select the Role name menu choice. This will add a role name called thePayClerk to the diagram.
3. While the role name is still selected, enter its name . . . myClerk.

**MAKE THE ASSOCIATION PRIVATE**

1. Right-click on the association near the Payclerk class to make the shortcut menu visible.
2. Select the Private menu choice.

**SET THE MULTIPLICITY**

1. Right-click on the association near the Payclerk class to make the shortcut menu visible.
2. Select the Multiplicity:1 menu choice.

**USE THE MODEL ASSISTANT TO SET CODE GENERATION PROPERTIES FOR THE IPAYROLL INTERFACE**

1. Right-click on the IPayroll class on the class diagram or in the Browser to make the shortcut menu visible.
2. Select the Model Assistant menu choice.
3. Select IPayroll in the Model Assistant tree view.
4. Click the arrow in the Instancing field to make the drop-down menu visible.
5. Select MultiUse.
6. Click the OK button to close the Model Assistant.

**USE THE MODEL ASSISTANT TO SET CODE GENERATION PROPERTIES FOR THE PAYROLL CLASS**

1. Right-click on the Payroll class on the class diagram or in the Browser to make the shortcut menu visible.
2. Select the Model Assistant menu choice.
3. Select Payroll in the Model Assistant tree view.
4. Click the arrow in the Instancing field to make the drop-down menu visible.
5. Select MultiUse.
6. Click the + next to the Implements Classes package in the tree view to expand the view.
7. Click the + next to IPayroll in the tree view to expand the view.
8. Select the IPayroll_calcPay operation.
9. Select the Public radio button in the Access field.
10. Click the + next to the Properties package in the tree view to expand the view.
11. Click the + next to myClerk in the tree view to expand the view.
12. Select myClerk.
13. Click the New checkbox.
14. Click the OK button to close the Model Assistant.

**CREATE THE PAYROLLCALCULATOR COMPONENT**

1. Right-click on the Component View package in the Browser to make the shortcut menu visible.
2. Select the New: Component menu choice. This will add a component called NewComponent to the Browser.
3. While the new component is still selected, enter its name . . . PayrollCalculator.

**ASSIGN A STEREOTYPE TO THE PAYROLL**

1. Right-click on the PayrollCalculator component in the Browser to make the shortcut menu visible.
2. Select the Open Specification menu choice.
3. Click the arrow in the Stereotype field to make the drop-down menu visible.
4. Select ActiveX DLL.
5. Click the OK button to close the Component Specification.

**ADD THE COMPONENT TO THE MAIN COMPONENT DIAGRAM**

1. Double-click on the diagram called Main in the Component View package of the Browser to open the diagram.
2. Click to select the PayrollCalculator component in the Browser and drag it onto the diagram.

**ASSIGN THE CLASSES TO THE PAYROLLCALCULATOR COMPONENT**

1. Double-click on the Payroll component on the diagram or in the Browser to make the Component Specification visible.
2. Select the Realizes tab.
3. Click to select the IPayroll class.
4. Press the Shift button.
5. Click to select the Payroll class.
6. Click to select the Payclerk class.
7. Right-click to make the pop-up menu visible.
8. Select the Assign menu choice.
9. Click the OK button to close the Component specification.

**GENERATE THE VISUAL BASIC CODE**

1.  Click to select the PayrollCalculator component on the Component Diagram.
2.  Select the Tools:Visual Basic:Update code menu choice to make the Code Update tool visible.
3.  Select the Finish button on the Code Update tool.
4.  You will be prompted to save the model. Enter PayrollCalculator in the Filename field and click the Save button.
5.  When the code generation is complete, the Summary window is displayed. Click the Close button to close the Code Update tool.

**ADD THE METHOD CODE FOR THE PAYCLERK CLASS**

1.  In Visual Basic, go to the calcPay method of the Payclerk class.
2.  Add the following code:
    calcPay = rate * 40
3.  In Visual Basic, go to the IPayroll_calcPay method of the Payroll class.
4.  Add the following code:
    IPayroll_calcPay = myClerk.calcPay(rate)
5.  Select the Project:PayrollCalculator Properties menu choice.
6.  Click the arrow in the Startup Object field to make the drop-down menu visible.
7.  Select (None).
8.  Click the OK button to close the Project Properties window.
9.  Select the File:Make PayrollCalculator.dll . . . menu choice.
10. Click the OK button in the Make Project window to save the new dll.
11. Select the File:Exit menu choice to exit Visual Basic (you do not have to save the files).

## REUSE THE ACTIVEX DLL

WE WILL NOW use this DLL in another application by walking through the analysis and design steps recommended in this book. To set the stage: You are tasked with building an application that will display the pay for an employee. The user of the application is the Manager. You must use the DLL provided by the payroll department (DLL created earlier). Start with a new, empty model.

### CREATE THE USE CASE DIAGRAM

1.  Create a new model. Do not use a framework.
2.  Open the Main use case diagram by clicking the + next to the Use Case View package in the Browser to expand the package and double-clicking on the diagram called Main.
3.  Click to select the Actor icon on the toolbar and click on the diagram to place the actor.
4.  While the new actor is still selected, enter its name . . . Manager.
5.  Right-click on the actor on the use case diagram to make the shortcut menu visible.
6.  Select the Options:Stereotype Display:Icon menu choice.
7.  Click to select the Use Case icon on the toolbar and click on the diagram to place the use case.
8.  While the new use case is still selected, enter its name . . . Display Pay.
9.  Click to select the Unidirectional Association icon on the toolbar, click on the Manager actor, and drag the line to the Display Pay use case.

### CREATE A REALIZATIONS USE CASE DIAGRAM

1.  Right-click on the Logical View package in the Browser to make the pop-up menu visible.
2.  Select the New:UseCaseDiagram menu choice. This will add a use case diagram called NewDiagram to the Browser.
3.  While the new diagram is still selected, enter its name . . . Realizations.
4.  Double-click on the Realizations use case diagram to open the diagram.

### CREATE THE REALIZATION USE CASE

1. Click to select the Use Case icon on the toolbar and click on the use case diagram to place the object. This will add a use case called NewUseCase to the diagram.
2. Double-click on the use case to open the Specification.
3. Enter the name Display Pay in the Name field. (Note: It is important that you name the use case in this manner so the namespace support in Rose is invoked. *Do not* name the use case using the diagram. If you do so, Rose assumes that you want the Display Pay use case from the Use Case View).
4. Click the arrow in the Stereotype field to make the drop-down menu visible.
5. Select use-case-realization.
6. Click the OK button to close the Specification.
7. You will be informed that the use case Display Pay now exists in multiple namespaces. This is okay. Click the OK button to close the Warning window.
8. Right-click on the use case to make the shortcut menu visible.
9. Select the Stereotype Display:Icon menu choice.

### CREATE A SEQUENCE DIAGRAM

1. Right-click on the Display Pay realization use case in the Browser to make the pop-up menu visible.
2. Select the New:Sequence Diagram menu choice.
3. While the new sequence diagram is still selected, enter its name . . . Display Pay for an Employee.
4. Double-click on the new sequence diagram in the Browser to open the diagram.

**ADD OBJECTS AND MESSAGES TO THE SEQUENCE DIAGRAM**

1. Click to select the Manager actor in the Browser and drag the actor onto the sequence diagram.
2. Click to select the Object icon on the toolbar and click on the sequence diagram to place the object.
3. While the object is still selected, enter its name . . . aPay-Form.
4. Click to select the Object Message icon on the toolbar, click on the dashed line for the actor, and drag the message to the dashed line for the aPayForm object.
5. While the new message is still selected, enter its name . . . display pay for joe.
6. Click to select the Object icon on the toolbar and click on the sequence diagram to place the object.
7. While the object is still selected, enter its name . . . Joe.
8. Click to select the Object Message icon on the toolbar, click on the dashed line for the aPayForm, and drag the message to the dashed line for the Joe object.
9. While the new message is still selected, enter its name . . . get pay rate.
10. Click to select the Object icon on the toolbar and click on the sequence diagram to place the object.
11. While the object is still selected, enter its name . . . aPay-Clerk.
12. Click to select the Object Message icon on the toolbar, click on the dashed line for the aPayForm, and drag the message to the dashed line for the aPayClerk object.
13. While the new message is still selected, enter its name . . . calculate pay for this rate.
14. Click to select the Message to Self icon on the toolbar and click on the dashed line for the aPayForm object to place the message.
15. While the message is still selected, enter its name . . . display pay.

**CREATE THE PAYROLLFORM CLASS AND THE EMPLOYEE CLASS**

1. Right-click on the Logical View package in the Browser to make the pop-up menu visible.
2. Select the New:Class menu choice.
3. While the new class is still selected, enter its name . . . PayrollForm.
4. Right-click on the PayrollForm class in the Browser to make the pop-up menu visible.
5. Select the Open Specification menu command.
6. Click the arrow in the Stereotype field to make the drop-down menu visible.
7. Select the Form stereotype. (Note: If you did not set the default language to Visual Basic, this stereotype will not be available. You can either delete the class, set the default language to Visual Basic and re-create the class, or wait until you assign the class to a component with the language set to Visual Basic to add the stereotype).
8. Click the OK button to close the Specification.
9. Click to select the PayrollForm class in the Browser and enter its documentation in the Documentation Window . . . this form displays the weekly pay for an employee.
10. Right-click on the Logical View package in the Browser to make the pop-up menu visible.
11. Select the New:Class menu choice.
12. While the new class is still selected, enter its name . . . Employee.
13. While the new class is still selected, enter its documentation in the Documentation window . . . an Employee is someone who is paid by the Company.

**ADD THE DLL TO THE MODEL**

1. Click the + next to the Component View package in the Browser to expand the package.
2. Double-click on the component diagram called Main to open the diagram.
3. Open the Windows Explorer and find the PayrollCalculator.dll created earlier.
4. Select the PayrollCalculator.dll and drag it onto the open component diagram.
5. Select the Full Import menu choice.

**ASSIGN THE OBJECTS IN THE SEQUENCE DIAGRAM TO CLASSES**

1. If the Display Pay for an Employee sequence diagram is not open, right-click on the sequence diagram in the Browser to make the pop-up menu visible and select the Open menu choice.
2. Click the + next to the Logical View package in the Browser to expand the package.
3. Click to select the PayrollForm class and drag it onto the aPayForm object. Ignore the warning.
4. Click to select the Employee class and drag it onto the Joe object. Ignore the warning.
5. Click the + next to the COM package in the Logical View package of the Browser to expand the package.
6. Click the + next to the PayrollCalculator package in the Logical View package of the Browser to expand the package.
7. Click to select the Payroll class and drag it onto the aPayClerk object. Ignore the warning.

### ASSIGN MESSAGES TO OPERATIONS

Note: The messages to the form class are not operations. They will become fields on the form and we will set them in Visual Basic.

1. Right-click on the get pay rate message and select the < new operation > menu choice. This will open the Operation Specification.
2. Enter the name of the operation in the Name field . . . getRate.
3. Click the arrow in the Return Class field to make the drop-down menu visible.
4. Select Currency. (As before, if you did not set the default language to Visual Basic, Currency will not be a choice.)
5. Click the OK button to close the Specification.
6. Right-click on the calculate pay for this rate message to make the pop-up menu visible.
7. Select IPayroll_calcPay.

### CREATE A CLASS DIAGRAM

1. Click the + next to the Logical View package in the Browser to expand the package.
2. Double-click on the diagram called Main to open the diagram.
3. Select the Query:Add Classes menu choice.
4. By default, the package is the Logical View package.
5. Click the All > > button to add the PayrollForm and the Employee classes to the diagram.
6. Click the arrow in the Package field to make the drop-down menu visible.
7. Select the PayrollCalculator package.
8. Select the All > > button to add the classes to the diagram.
9. Click the OK button to close the Add Classes window.
10. Click the Unidirectional Association icon on the toolbar, click on the PayrollForm class, and drag the association line to the Employee class.

11. Right-click on the association line near the Employee class to make the pop-up menu visible.

12. Select the Role name menu choice and enter the role name . . . anEmployee.

13. Right-click on the association line near the Employee class to make the pop-up menu visible.

14. Select the Multiplicity:1 menu choice.

15. Click the Unidirectional Association icon on the toolbar, click on the PayrollForm class, and drag the association line to the Payroll class. (stereotype = coclass).

16. Right-click on the association line near the Payroll class to make the pop-up menu visible.

17. Select the Role Name menu choice and enter the role name . . . myPayClerk.

18. Right-click on the association line near the Payroll class to make the pop-up menu visible.

19. Select the Multiplicity:1 menu choice.

**USE THE MODEL ASSISTANT TO SET CODE GENERATION OPTIONS**

1. Right-click on the PayrollForm class to make the pop-up menu visible.

2. Select the Model Assistant menu choice.

3. Click the + next to anEmployee property to expand the tree.

4. Select the anEmployee data member.

5. Click to select the New checkbox.

6. Click the + next to myPayClerk property to expand the tree.

7. Select the myPayClerk data member.

8. Click to select the New checkbox.

9. Click the OK button to close the Model Assistant.

**CREATE THE COMPONENT DIAGRAM**

1. Click the + next to the Component View package in the Browser to expand the package.
2. Double-click on the diagram called Main to open the diagram.
3. Click to select the Package icon on the toolbar and click on the diagram to place the package.
4. While the package is still selected, enter its name . . . Manager Options.
5. Click the + next to the COM package in the Component View of the Browser to expand the package.
6. Click to select the PayrollCalculator package in the component view of the Browser and drag the package onto the Main component diagram.
7. Click to select the Dependency icon on the toolbar, click on the Manager Options package, and drag the dependency line to the PayrollCalculator package.
8. Double-click on the Manager Options package on the component diagram to open the Main component diagram for the package.
9. Click to select the Component icon on the toolbar and click on the diagram to place the component.
10. Double-click on the component on the diagram to open the Specification.
11. Enter the name of the component in the Name field . . . DisplayPay.
12. If you did not set the default language to Visual Basic, then click the arrow in the Language field to make the drop-down menu visible and select Visual Basic.
13. Click the arrow in the stereotype field to make the drop-down menu visible.
14. Select the Standard EXE stereotype.
15. Click the OK button to close the Specification.
16. Select the PayrollForm class in the Logical View package in the Browser and drag the class onto the DisplayPay component.
17. Select the Employee class in the Logical View package in the Browser and drag the class onto the DisplayPay component.

18. Click the + next to the PayrollCalculator package in the Component View of the Browser to expand the package.
19. Click to select the PayrollCalculator component in the Browser and drag it onto the component diagram.
20. Click to select the Dependency icon on the toolbar, click on the DisplayPay component, and drag the dependency line to the PayrollCalculator component.

### GENERATE THE CODE

1. Click to select the DisplayPay component.
2. Select the Tools:VisualBasic:UpdateCode menu choice to make the Code Update tool visible.
3. Click the Finish button.
4. Click the Close button to close the Code Update tool.

### IMPLEMENT THE CODE IN VISUAL BASIC

1. Select the Employee class.
2. Enter the following implementation code for the getRate method:

    getRate = 10

3. Select the PayrollForm class.
4. Place a Text Box on the form.
5. Enter the following implementation code for the Form_Load method:

    Dim theRate As Integer
    theRate = anEmployee.getRate
    Text1.Text = myPayClerk.IPayroll_calcPay(theRate)

6. Select the Project: Display Pay Properties . . . menu choice.
7. Click the arrow in the StartUp Object field to make the drop-down menu visible.
8. Select PayrollForm.
9. Click the OK button to close the Properties window.
10. Run the executable and you will see 400 displayed in the textbox.

# Glossary

*ACTION*

Behavior that accompanies a transition event. An action is considered to take zero time and cannot be interrupted.

*ACTIVITY*

Behavior that occurs while in a state. An activity can be interrupted by a transition event.

*ACTOR*

Someone or something external to the system that must interact with the system under development.

*AGGREGATION*

A stronger form of an association where the relationship is between a whole and its part(s).

*ARCHITECTURE*

The logical and physical structure of a system, forged by all the strategic and tactical design decisions applied during development.

*ASSOCIATION*

A bidirectional, semantic connection between two classes.

*ASSOCIATION CLASS*

A class that holds information belonging to a link between two objects and not with one object alone.

*ATTRIBUTE*

A data definition held by objects of a class. The structure of the class.

*AUTOMATIC TRANSITION*

Transition that occurs automatically after the activity within the originating state is completed.

*BACKGROUND PROBLEM STATEMENT*

Cumulative background material assembled before working on a project. It often includes a description and critique of the previous system.

*BASE PROJECT*

A project that supplements the information in a program-specific project, usually with information about header files for compiler specific libraries or other class libraries being used.

*BUSINESS GOALS*

Prioritized statements of the organization's needs used to guide decision making and tradeoff throughout the development process.

*CLASS*

A description of a group of objects with common properties (attributes), common behavior (operations), common relationships to other objects (associations and aggregations), and common semantics.

*CLASS DIAGRAM*

A view or picture of some or all of the classes in a model.

*CLASS LIBRARY*

A library consisting of classes that may be used by other developers.

*COLLABORATION DIAGRAM*

A diagram that shows object interactions organized around the objects and their links to each other.

*COMPONENT DIAGRAM*

A diagram that shows the organizations and dependencies among software components, including source code components, run-time components, and executable components.

*CONSISTENCY CHECKING*

The process of ensuring that information in both the static view of the system (class diagrams) and the dynamic view of the system (sequence and collaboration diagrams) are telling the same story.

*CONSTRUCTION*

Building the product as a series of incremental iterations.

*CONTROLLED UNIT*

A package that can be loaded or saved independently and integrated into a configuration management system.

*DECISION POINT*

A point in an activity diagram where guard conditions are used to indicate different possible transitions.

*DEPLOYMENT DIAGRAM*

A diagram used to show the allocation of processes to nodes in the physical design of a system.

*DESIGN*

How the system will be realized in the implementation phase.

*ELABORATION*

Planning the necessary activities and required resources; specifying the features and designing the architecture.

*GENERALIZATION*

Process used to create superclasses that encapsulate structure and behavior common to several classes.

*GUARD*

A condition that must evaluate to TRUE in order for a specified transition to occur.

*IMPLEMENTATION*

> The production of the code that will result in an executable system.

*INCEPTION*

> The specification of the project vision.

*INHERITANCE*

> A relationship among classes, where one class shares the structure and/or behavior defined in one or more other classes.

*ITERATION PLAN*

> Schedule of the iterative releases planned for a system.

*ITERATIVE AND INCREMENTAL LIFE CYCLE*

> Development of a series of architectural releases that evolve into the final system.

*KEY MECHANISM*

> A design decision that has local architectural implications.

*LAYER*

> The collection of packages at the same level of abstraction.

*MODEL*

> An abstraction that portrays the essentials of a complex problem or structure, making it easier to manipulate.

*OBJECT*

> A concept, abstraction, or thing with sharp boundaries and meaning for an application.

*OPERATION*

> Work that one object performs upon another in order to elicit a reaction. The behavior of the class.

*PARTITION*
> The packages that form a part of a given level of abstraction.

*POLYMORPHISM*
> Provides the capability for clients to manipulate objects in terms of their common superclasses.

*PROOF OF CONCEPT PROTOTYPE*
> Prototype used to validate the initial assumptions stated for a given problem space.

*REQUIREMENTS ANALYSIS*
> Description of what the system should do.

*SCENARIO*
> An instance of a use case—it is one path through the flow of events for the use case.

*SEQUENCE DIAGRAM*
> A diagram that depicts object interactions arranged in time sequence.

*SPECIALIZATION*
> Process used to create subclasses that represent refinements in which structure and/or behavior are added, modified, or even hidden.

*STATE*
> The cumulative results of the behavior of an object; one of the possible conditions in which an object may exist.

*STATE TRANSITION*
> The passing from one state to another state.

*STATECHART DIAGRAM*

Diagram used to show the state space of a given class, the events that cause a transition from one state to another, and the actions that result from a state change.

*STEREOTYPE*

A new type of modeling element that extends the metamodel. Stereotypes must be based on elements that are part of the UML metamodel.

*SUBCLASS*

A class that inherits from one or more classes.

*SUPERCLASS*

The class from which another class inherits.

*SWIMLANE*

A partition on activity diagrams for organizing responsibilities for activities. They often correspond to organizational units in a business model.

*SYNCHRONIZATION BAR*

Horizontal or vertical bars that show activities that may be done concurrently. Synchronization bars are also used to show joins in the workflow.

*TEST*

The verification of the entire system.

*TRANSITION*

Supplying the product to the user community (manufacturing, delivering, and training).

*UNIFIED MODELING LANGUAGE (UML)*

A language used to specify, visualize, and document the artifacts of an object-oriented system under development.

*USE CASE*

> Representation of the business processes of the system. The model of a dialogue between an actor and the system.

*USE CASE DIAGRAM*

> A graphical representation of some or all of the actors, use cases, and their interactions.

*USE CASE MODEL*

> The collection of actors, use cases, and use case diagrams for a system.

*VISUAL MODELING*

> A way of thinking about problems using models organized around real-world ideas.

# Index

# Rational Minds and Addison-Wesley Authors— What a Combination!

DEVELOPING ENTERPRISE JAVA APPLICATIONS WITH J2EE AND UML
KHAWAR ZAMAN AHMED
CARY E. UMRYSH
0-201-73829-5

USE CASE MODELING
KURT BITTNER
IAN SPENCE
0-201-70913-9

OBJECT-ORIENTED ANALYSIS AND DESIGN WITH APPLICATIONS
GRADY BOOCH
SECOND EDITION
0-8053-5340-2

OBJECT SOLUTIONS
MANAGING THE OBJECT-ORIENTED PROJECT
GRADY BOOCH
0-8053-0594-7

THE UNIFIED MODELING LANGUAGE USER GUIDE
GRADY BOOCH
JAMES RUMBAUGH
IVAR JACOBSON
The ultimate tutorial to the UML from the original designers
0-201-57168-4

Software Leadership
A Guide to Successful Software Development
Murray Cantor
0-201-70044-1

BUILDING WEB APPLICATIONS WITH UML SECOND EDITION
JIM CONALLEN
0-201-73038-3

BUILDING J2EE APPLICATIONS WITH THE RATIONAL UNIFIED PROCESS
PETER EELES
KELLI HOUSTON
WOJTEK KOZACZYNSKI
0-201-79166-8

IVAR JACOBSON
THE OBJECT ADVANTAGE
BUSINESS PROCESS REENGINEERING WITH OBJECT TECHNOLOGY
0-201-42289-1

Object-Oriented Software Engineering
A Use Case Driven Approach
0-201-54435-0

SOFTWARE REUSE
Architecture, Process and Organization for Business Success
0-201-92476-5

THE UNIFIED SOFTWARE DEVELOPMENT PROCESS
IVAR JACOBSON
GRADY BOOCH
JAMES RUMBAUGH
The complete guide to the Unified Process from the original designers
0-201-57169-2

THE RATIONAL UNIFIED PROCESS AN INTRODUCTION SECOND EDITION
PHILIPPE KRUCHTEN
0-201-70710-1

MANAGING SOFTWARE REQUIREMENTS
A UNIFIED APPROACH
DEAN LEFFINGWELL
DON WIDRIG
0-201-61593-2

UML FOR DATABASE DESIGN
ERIC J. NAIBURG
ROBERT A. MAKSIMCHUK
Foreword by Grady Booch
0-201-72163-5

VISUAL MODELING WITH RATIONAL ROSE 2002 AND UML
TERRY QUATRANI
Foreword by Grady Booch
0-201-72932-6

SOFTWARE PROJECT MANAGEMENT
A Unified Framework
WALKER ROYCE
Foreword by Barry Boehm
0-201-30958-0

THE UNIFIED MODELING LANGUAGE REFERENCE MANUAL
JAMES RUMBAUGH
IVAR JACOBSON
GRADY BOOCH
The definitive reference to the UML from the original designers
0-201-30998-X

SOFTWARE CONFIGURATION MANAGEMENT STRATEGIES AND RATIONAL CLEARCASE
A PRACTICAL INTRODUCTION
BRIAN A. WHITE
Foreword by Geoffrey M. Clemm
0-201-60478-7

For more information on these books by Rational Software Corporation employees, please go to **www.awprofessional.com**

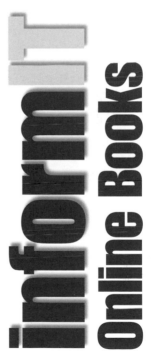